R. GUPTA'S

I0016446

Latest
ESSAYS
&
LETTERS

Highly Useful Book for Students, Readers &
Candidates Appearing for Competitive Exams

Compiled by
RPH Editorial Board

RAMESH PUBLISHING HOUSE, New Delhi

Published by
O.P. Gupta *for* Ramesh Publishing House
Admin. Office
12-H, New Daryaganj Road, Opp. Officers Mess,
New Delhi-110002 ℑ 23261567, 23275224

E-mail: info@rameshpublishinghouse.com
Website: www.rameshpublishinghouse.com
Showroom
● Balaji Market, Nai Sarak, Delhi-6 ℑ 23253720, 23282525
● 4457, Nai Sarak, Delhi-6, ℑ 23918938

Book Code: R-1094

14th Edition: 1911

ISBN: 978-81-7812-805-4

HSN Code: 49011010

CONTENTS

CURRENT TOPICS

SECTION A : ESSAYS

A. GLORIOUS SOCIAL FESTIVALS

B. NATIONAL FESTIVALS

3

C. PHILANTHROPIC CHARACTER (PERSONALITIES)

D. THE MAN OF LETTERS/LITERARY/SPORTS PERSONALITIES

E. NATIONAL LEADER OR NATION BUILDER

F. HISTORICAL PERSONALITIES

G. MUSICAL MAESTRO

H. THE GREAT SCIENTISTS

I. SOCIAL ASPECTS/ISSUES

J. EVOLUTION/SPLENDOUR OF SCIENCE

K. PLACES OF REPUTE/HERITAGE/MONUMENT

7

SECTION B : LETTERS

_____

CURRENT TOPICS

INDIA AS EMERGING SUPERPOWER

From an average country in 1947 when India got freedom to an emerging superpower in 2019, our country has accomplished a position of respect among the leading powers of the world like the US, Russia, China and other European countries. India's workforce, its strategic location, its resources and military, technological advancement and nuclear asset – all these certainly put India in an emerging superpower category. With good relations with Middle East countries, except with Pakistan, India has exerted good influence on the west side while on eastern borders, better relations with Bangladesh, Bhutan and Myanmar have helped create a prestigious position of the country. While southern side is not a problem, north offers China to compete and during Doklam conflict India did well to confront Beijing.

Relations with other countries show the strength and weakness of a nation; India has done well in developing close relationships with the world powers like the US, EU, Japan, Russia and the Middle East countries. Our foreign relation is on a better plane with the African Union particularly South Africa, Israel, Australia and South American nations, especially Brazil. India has significantly enhanced its prestige and image among the western countries as a free and democratic country, which paved the way for the signing of a civilian nuclear deal with the US in March 2006. The most important part of India's engagement with the world is its advocacy of Non-Aligned Movement, and at the same time maintaining good relationships with Russia and the US. India played a powerful role in South Asian affairs, for example, sending Indian Peace Keeping Force in the Bangladesh Liberation War and in Sri Lanka. As an active member of the Commonwealth and the WTO, India has worked hard to secure its own rights as well as those of other developing countries.

The one asset – population – can be either a boon or bane which way the teeming millions tilt, but the good point is the young population of India compared to more developed nations. It has approximately

65 per cent of its population below the age of 35. This workforce is an advantage in developing the country. Another plus point which helps India become a power is about 35 million Indians living across the globe, the socio-economically successful population especially in the US and Europe. The economy progress is one area which puts a nation in the lead; it is the economic growth of the US that allowed it to become military power. Right now Indian economy is the world's third largest in terms of real GDP after the US and China, overtaking the Japanese economy. According to the World Bank India overtook China to become the fastest-growing major economy in the world as of 2015.

English and IT skills are the great advantage of India; some have begun to describe India as a technology superpower. This is mainly due to the availability of a large pool of highly skilled, low cost, English speaking workforce. As the knowledge economy, India is becoming one of the world's leading producers of computer software and has witnessed a steady revolution in science and technology. India's rising scientific endeavours is that it was the 3rd nation to found a National Space Agency called ISRO after the USSR and the US. It was the third Asian nation to send satellites into space after China and Japan in 1970, starting with Aryabhatta in 1975. In January 2007, India became the fourth nation to complete atmospheric re-entry. If in October 2008 India launched its first unmanned lunar probe, Chandrayaan I, the lunar probe, in 2019 it sent Chandrayaan II to the Moon orbit. On 24 September 2014 India became the fourth nation to have a satellite orbiting Mars. India is the first Asian nation to achieve this and the first to do so in its first try.

In energy sector, India has achieved self-sufficiency. At present, India is constructing nine civilian nuclear power reactors and several hydro-power stations. Recently it also made a civilian nuclear energy deal with the US and EU. In the future, the world is expected to exit the fossil fuel age, and perhaps the nuclear energy age", and enter the renewable-energy age for which India is well prepared. With energy infrastructure is one area India has done extremely well by building roads, rail networks, bridges, airports, and dams. India is in the process of developing modern mass rapid transit systems to replace its existing system which is seen as inadequate to cater to present and future urban requirements. Metro rail system in Delhi, Mumbai, Chennai, Bangalore, Kolkata, Hyderabad, Kochi, Jaipur and Lucknow is the sign of development.

The pride of the nation is Indian Armed Forces, the military might of our country. The total armed forces of India are 2,414,700 strong. India possesses the second largest armed force in the world after China and the world's third largest defence force. Both in personnel and military equipment including fighter jets and missiles India has formidable power and is ready to meet any military power in the world. The Indian Air Force is the fourth largest air force in the world while Indian Navy is the world's fifth largest navy. India's Prithvi and Agni ballistic missiles, surface to air missiles Trishul and Akash and also the anti-tank Nag missile are the proof of our defence preparation. India is self-reliant in missile technology while our nuclear weapons exhibit our commitment to becoming, like the US and other superpowers, a superpower on earth.

RAM WINS, RAHIM DOESN'T LOSE

A Constitution Bench of the Supreme Court on November 9, 2019 permitted the construction of a temple at the site where the Babri Masjid once stood, and asked the government to allot a "prominent and suitable" five-acre plot for Muslims to construct a mosque in Ayodhya.

In a unanimous judgment, a Bench headed by Chief Justice of India Ranjan Gogoi asked the Centre, which had acquired the entire 67.73 acres of land including the 2.77 acre of the disputed Ramjanmabhumi-Babri Masjid premises in 1993, to formulate a scheme within three months and set up a trust to manage the property and construct a temple. For the time being, the possession of the disputed property would continue to vest with the Centre until a notification is issued by it investing the property in the trust.

The Bench also directed that the Sunni Central Waqf Board should be given a five-acre plot, either by the Centre from within its acquired area, or by the Uttar Pradesh government "at a suitable, prominent place in Ayodhya". The Board would be at liberty to construct a mosque there. This should be done simultaneously with the transfer of the property to the proposed trust.

The judges declared that the demolition of the 16th century Babri Masjid on December 6, 1992, was "an egregious violation of the rule of law" and "a calculated act of destroying a place of public worship". The Muslims have been wrongly deprived of a mosque which had been constructed well over 450 years ago, the Bench said.

The Court referred to the Places of Worship (Special Provisions) Act of 1991, which prohibits the conversion of the status of any place of worship, to say that all religions are equal. "The Constitution does not make a distinction between the faith and belief of one religion and another. All forms of belief, worship and prayer are equal," Chief Justice Gogoi said, reading excerpts from the judgment for the Bench, also comprising Justices S.A. Bobde, D.Y. Chandrachud, Ashok Bhushan and S. Abdul Nazeer.

The court concluded that the Muslims were ousted from the 1500 square yards of the mosque through acts of damage during communal riots in 1934, desecration in the intervening night of December 22-23 of 1949 when idols were place inside the mosque, and finally, the demolition of the mosque in 1992.

"This court in the exercise of its powers under Article 142 of the Constitution must ensure that a wrong committed must be remedied. Justice would not prevail if the Court were to overlook the entitlement of the Muslims who have been deprived of the structure of the mosque through means which should not have been employed in a secular nation committed to the rule of law," Chief Justice Gogoi read out from the judgment.

The Supreme Court said the Allahabad High Court's remedy of a three-way bifurcation of the disputed premises among the Ayodhya deity, Sri Bhagwan Ram Virajman, Nirmohi Akhara and the Sunni Central Waqf Board "defied logic". It did not "secure a lasting sense of peace and tranquillity".

The judgment nevertheless concluded that the Sunni Central Waqf Board was unable to prove its claim of exclusive title and continuous possession of the disputed site. "The Muslims have offered no evidence to indicate that they were in exclusive possession of the inner structure prior to 1857 since the date of the construction in the sixteenth century," the court observed. On the other hand, the court held there was both oral and documentary evidence to support the Hindus' faith that the Janma Asthan was located where the Babri Masjid was constructed. It was beyond the ken of the court to probe whether this belief was justified. Judges cannot indulge in theology, but restrict themselves to evidence and balance of probabilities.

The court said there was proof of extensive worship offered by the Hindus, especially in the outer courtyard where the Ram Chabutra and Sita Rasoi are located, even before the annexation of the Oudh by the British in 1857. The Hindus' possession of the outer courtyard has been established.

Besides, the Supreme Court accepted the version of the Archaeological Survey of India (ASI) that the mosque was not constructed on a vacant land. The ASI had suggested the remains of a large pre-existing structure underneath the Babri mosque which was "non-Islamic" in nature. The ASI had said the artefacts collected from the dig and the pillars of the mosque were of a non-Islamic origin.

The court refrained from arriving at a conclusion on the issue whether the pre-existing structure was demolished to construct the mosque. It said the ASI had also maintained a studied silence, only venturing that the pre-existing structure was used to build the mosque. The court, however, dismissed the contention raised by the Hindu side that the land, Ram Janam Asthan, was a legal personality just as the minor Ayodhya deity, Ram Lala, was. The court said this claim was a "mirror image" of the Muslim's claim that the disputed site was waqf property.

The court dismissed the Akhara's petition as time-barred. and rejected its suit claiming shebaiti (managerial rights) over the property. However, the court invoked its extraordinary powers to ask the government to give Nirmohi Akhara, considering the sect's historical presence at the disputed site, to provide it with an "appropriate role in the management" of the property.

KASHMIR : PARADISE REGAINED

The special status accorded to Jammu & Kashmir under Article 370 of the Constitution has been removed with the presidential notification of 5 August 2019. This is a bold move by the government reflecting strong political will. The Constitution of India will, from now on, fully apply to Jammu & Kashmir, and any special exceptions previously provided to the latter, are ended.

Where is Kashmir in the metric of India's development? Deng Xiaoping said that development is the hard truth. A young Kashmiri told a few months ago her birthplace was in the "stone age"; that in terms of economic development, Kashmir was two hundred years behind the rest of India. If one is asked what Kashmir needs most today, it is not the "azadi" that some young Kashmiris claim, but investment, modernisation, liveli-hoods, gender empowerment and development.

The bold step by the government was preceded by a controversial shroud of secrecy inducing a sense of doom and gloom in the Kashmir Valley. Some Kashmiri leaders wrongly stated that Article 370 was the only reason for Kashmiri's "connection" with India. The Instrument of Accession signed by Maharaja Hari Singh in October 1947 tied Kashmir to India. Article 3 of the Constitution of Jammu & Kashmir of November 1956 clearly stated that the state "is and shall be an integral part of the Union of India". It was stipulated that the said Article 3 could not be amended or changed.

The erstwhile princely state of Jammu & Kashmir acceded to the then Dominion of India in October 1947 against the backdrop of attacks

☆☆ *Latest Essays & Letters* ☆☆

by raiders from Pakistan. Even as the government took subsequent steps, after these attacks by raiders from Pakistan. Even as the government took subsequent steps, after these attacks were quelled, to ensure a special status for Kashmir, the view that strengthened across the public imagery and mainstream political spectrum was that the state was an irrevocable constituent of the Indian Union meriting no special status, that the Union retained absolute sovereignty and paramountcy over it.

The Union of India is permanent and indestructible, as the founding father of our Constitution, Babasaheb Ambedkar, stated. The instinct of the central government has always been to seek, as Ambedkar said, "uniformity in all the basic matters which are essential to maintain the unity of the country". Ambedkar saw the country as an integrated whole, and its people a single people living "under a single imperium derived from a single source". The government of Narendra Modi obviously does not hold a different view.

Even as innocent Kashmiri lives have been lost in the violence of the last decades, the defence of Kashmir against aggression and against terrorism has involved the loss of lives of Indians in uniform from every part of India (most recently in Pulwama) in the cause of national unity, a fact that cannot be ignored by any government elected to power by popular vote across the nation.

The wages of endless conflict coupled with terrorism fuelled by groups operating from Pakistan across India, have hardened Indian opinion. The popular mood is not for conciliation towards Pakistan or secessionist, radical groups in the Valley. The government has seized the strategic opportunity to end special status for Kashmir knowing that the mood in the rest of the country will be largely supportive.

Jammu & Kashmir as defined in the 1956 Constitution includes the area under current occupation of Pakistan (as also the territories traded by Pakistan to China in 1963 and the area occupied by China in the Aksai Chin area of Ladakh). The geographical expanse of the erstwhile princely state is now in the physical grasp of three countries, India, Pakistan, and China.

Both Pakistan and China have protested the latest moves by the government of India after the presidential notification on Article 370. Pakistan's response was on expected lines. China's demarche on Ladakh recalls the protest made when Arunachal Pradesh was granted statehood in February 1987. The government of India is justified in rejecting these protests.

The two newly announced Union territories (now the direct administrative responsibility of the Centre) are of enormous strategic importance to India and to the defence of the Union. The fact that events in Afghanistan are fast approaching an outcome that will accommodate the pro-Pakistani Taliban, spelling increased Islamic radicalisation across borders, and enabling Islamabad to further fine tune cross-border terrorism against India as an instrument of state policy, cannot be ignored. The Trump administration's inclination to 'mediate' between India and Pakistan on Kashmir obviously at Pakistan's prodding, also demands that India take stock of her options on Kashmir with strategic foresight and devise a clear way forward.

For years, the Valley has preferred anger and alienation versus a pragmatic choice in favour of economic development and closer identification with India. For the government, the challenge in Kashmir is to ensure that the threats to security from cross-border forces and internal dissent are effectively addressed together with building trust and conviction that a brighter future of development, good governance, respect for fundamental rights, and job opportunities is assured for the people there. Kashmir must be drawn away from the precipice, with humane and judicious calibration, bringing the prodigal back into the family fold. We must borrow from both Kautilya and post-Kalinga Ashoka.

❏ ❏ ❏

SECTION A : ESSAYS

A
GLORIOUS SOCIAL FESTIVALS

DIWALI

A festival plays a great role as it brings new joy and hope to the people. Of all the festivals I like Diwali. Diwali or Deepawali which means rows of lights is an important festival not only of Hindus but of almost all the communities living in India. It is celebrated with great enthusiasm all over the country.

This festive day falls on the Amavasya of the month of Kartik every year exactly twenty days after Dussehra by the Hindu Calendar. This festival of lights, sweets and crackers is celebrated with fun and frolic by all. In this day, the return of Lord Rama to Ayodhya after gaining victory over Ravana is memorable. To welcome him back and to express their joy, the people of Ayodhya lighted rows of earthen lamps. Some others believe that Goddess Lakshmi of wealth and prosperity visits every house on this night. To welcome her the lights are lit throughout the night. Jains believe that in the early morning of this day Lord Mahavir attained 'Moksha or Salvation.'

The preparations start with cleaning their houses and shops. This is the best time for the manufacturers and sellers of sweets, toys and idols of gods and goddesses, crackers, candles etc. As people are eager to purchase new clothes, utensils, greeting cards and other things, there is great hustle-bustle in every market. These market areas are decorated and they undoubtedly draw a lot of crowd.

On the day of Diwali, everyone is happy and mirthful. Clad in new clothes they visit their friends and relatives. Sweets and greetings are exchanged.

17

At night people worship Lord Ganesh and Goddess Lakshmi with great devotion. People decorate their houses with illuminating lamps, candles and electric bulbs. The sight of these glittering lights is very enchanting as the night appears to be under the spell of a full moon. Children let off fireworks. All the variety of crackers like anars, rockets, lighting pencils, etc. is seen.

Fireworks must be under the supervision of elders as any folly can lead to injuries, burns and fire hazards. Many fire tenders are placed at different areas for ready help in case of need. All people, young and old, who take part in the happy occasion must be careful so that accidents of such harm do not occur.

Some people wrongly believe that they should gamble on the day of Diwali. Gambling is a social evil and people must keep away from this practice.

Diwali is the festival of wealth, prosperity and happiness. It is the festival celebrated by the majority of Indians in every nook and corner of the country. As such, it has become a symbol of unity in diversity.

HOLI

Holi is one of the important festivals of the Hindus. It is a colourful festival of great joy and enthusiasm. This festival is celebrated all over the country as a day filled with complete mischief, fun and enjoyment. Holi indicates the end of the winters and the beginning of the spring season. According to the Hindu Calendar it is celebrated on the full-moon night of the month of Phalgun.

Holi is celebrated to mark the victory of truth over evil, the victory of Prahlad over King Hiranyakashyap. Prahlad was a devotee of God. His father, King Hiranyakashyap did not believe in God but-believed in his own powers. He failed to deviate his son's devotion to God and decided to kill him by burning him alive. Hiranyakashyap's sister, Holika, had a God-gifted boon that she would not be burnt in the fire. She sat with her nephew in the blazing fire. But Holika herself was burnt and Prahlad survived unhurt. The truth, the powers of the Supreme God, defeated the false evil.

During the day, women folk worship a stack of wooden logs called Holi. At the end of the day in the full-moon night Holi is burnt in a holy way. The green ears of barley and gram are heated up in the fire and distributed among friends and relatives. New friendships are made and old enmities are forgotten.

Next day is the festive day of Holi. All hearts are filled with joy. Children throw coloured water on each other while the elder people apply 'gulal' or 'abir'. There are noisy scenes as little groups of children move from one locality to another exchanging holi greetings, singing songs and laughing at their own jokes. It is almost mid-day when people move indoors to freshen themselves.

Though this is a festival of brotherhood and unity, it has some disadvantages too. Some ill-minded people-take this day as a chance to take revenge. They use dirty mud water. Use of strong colours-harmful to the skin, charcoal and grease often create a serious quarrel. This leads to unnecessary enmity and spoils the charm of the festival.

People must understand that this festival is celebrated to bring people together to be happy. They must take care not to indulge in bad practices and make it one of the best festivals. Then they can enjoy to their maximum amidst the beautiful colours.

Let us observe Holi as festival of love, universal brotherhood and goodwill among individuals and communities.

DUSSEHRA

Dussehra, a ten day long festival is celebrated throughout the country with great religious beliefs. According to the Hindu Calendar this important festival of the Hindus falls in the second fortnight of the month of 'Ashwin'. It is the festival of victory and triumph, the victory of good over evil.

In Northern India, the life of Lord Rama is enacted as Ramlila for nine nights and on the tenth day the effigies of Ravana along with his brother Kumbhakarna and son Meghnad are burnt with a lot of fanfare. It is believed that in order to conquer Ravana, Rama had prayed to Goddess Durga for nine days and on the tenth, he succeeded in slaying

Ravana. Tools, weapons, cattle and books, which represent knowledge and learning are worshipped.

In North-East, particularly in Bengal, huge decorated idols of Goddess Durga are worshipped for nine days and immersed into the sea or river on the tenth day amidst religious chants. A variety of cultural programmes are also presented in the public pandals where Durga Pooja is held.

In the West, Goddess Saraswati is also worshipped along with Goddess Durga. Navratri is celebrated with nine nights of ras and garba dancing. On Dussehra day, the leaves of the 'shami' tree, referred to as gold, are presented to friends and relatives.

In Southern India, a wonderful display of dolls is the manner of celebrating Dussehra. A small pot known as 'Kalash' which symbolises the Goddess of strength and fertility is worshipped.

In big cities, however, all these rituals, customs and traditions have got mingled as everybody has a good time celebrating the festival in their own way. Even in this happy mix the importance of the festival remains and reminds the people that good shall always prevail over evil.

Let us celebrate Dussehra with a spirit of love and friendship for all.

RAKSHA BANDHAN

Sravani is an ancient Vedic festival traditionally associated with the Brahmins on which day they change their sacred thread. Both Raksha Bandhan and Sravani are celebrated on the full moon day in the month of Shravan (August). Raksha Bandhan, the more popular of the two festivals, is a Hindu sister's day when brothers and sisters reaffirm their bonds of affections.

Sisters tie colourful threads or rakhis on their brother's wrists. The brothers in turn promise to protect their sisters and give them gifts. Raksha Bandhan is celebrated in different forms in different areas and it is also known by the names like Rakhi and Saluno.

Now, Rakha Bandhan is very popular among the Hindu communities and it marks the affection between brothers and sisters.

ID-UL-FITR

Id-ul-Fitr is the festival of muslims and celebrated in all parts of the world. Id-ul-Fitr, popularly known as the 'Festival of the Breaking of the Fast', occurs as soon as the new moon is sighted at the end of the month of fasting, namely Ramazan. The festival is intended to be a festive and joyous occasion. Special foods and delicacies are prepared for the day and are distributed to neighbours and friends. Id-ul-Fitr is celebrated at the end of Ramzan, the Muslim month of fasting. It is an occasion of feasting and rejoicing.

The faithful muslims, wearing new clothes and caps, gather in the mosques to pray. Friends and relatives meet and exchange greetings. Prayers, family get-togethers and feasts are the major highlights of the festival.

Let us observe the festival with brotherhood and goodwill among individuals and communities.

CHRISTMAS

This festival is celebrated all over India, every year on 25th December and is devoted to Jesus Christ.

Christmas, the birth anniversary of Jesus Christ, is celebrated in India with great fervour all over India by the Christians. People decorate their houses, erect Christmas trees, make cribs with figures of baby Jesus, Mother Mary, Joseph, the three kings who come to visit the baby and shepherd boys and their herds grazing around, depicting the scenes of Jesus' birth in the Bible. They decorate the Christmas tree, hang stars, gifts and illuminate them.

On the Christmas day, people enjoy a sumptuous Christmas lunch. Christmas cakes and wine are served to visitors and gifts given to friends and relatives. Christmas celebrations vary in different parts of India. In some parts, small clay oil-burning lamps, mango leaves etc are used as Christmas decorations and mango and banana trees are decorated. All the major Indian cities wear a festive look. Shops and bazaars are decorated for the occasion and offer attractive bargains.

This is the most important and the merriest festival of the Christians. Other communities in India also look upon it as a festival of goodwill and greetings.

The day is spent in meeting friends and relatives. Greeting cards wishing joy and peace are exchanged. The night is enlivened with dances, carols and mid-night masses in all the churches. Youngsters dance hilariously on the streets singing carols to the accompaniment of musical instruments. The most popular carol is : "Silent night, holy night all is calm, all is bright round you Virgin Mother and Child Holy infant so tender and mild sleep in heavenly peace." Thus the Christmas season is rung in with a feeling of happiness and goodwill amidst the clouds of discontent.

It was only during the British period that the Christianity spread all over the country. The festival of Christmas is celebrated for ten continuous days. The end of these Christian festivities is commencing of the New year.

BAISAKHI

Baisakhi is a seasonal festival with a special accent. Though widely known all over India Baisakhi is originally celebrated in Punjab. This is the time when harvest is gathered in and the farmers are jubilant over fulfilment of their hard farming work. They are in mood of merry-making and walk miles to participate in Baisakhi fair. Since these fairs are also an expression of prosperity, singing and dancing constitute its most enchanting features.

The Punjab's famous dances of Bhangra and Giddha are inextricably linked with this festival. Many fairs in the Punjab are held near the tombs and shrines of pirs. These fairs must have originated in a spirit of devotion to those saints and sages. The most famous among such fairs are the Chhapar fair, the Jarag fair, and the Roshni fair of Jagranyan.

Baisakhi marks the beginning of the New Year, particularly in the northern part of India. It is one of the few Indian festivals that have a fixed date. Baisakhi comes on 13th April. In Kerala, Baisakhi is called as 'Vishu' and in Tamil Nadu, it is celebrated as 'Puthandu'. Being considered a holy day, the devout celebrate the Baisakhi with a dip in the holy rivers usually at dawn. It is on this day that Sun enters Aries, the first sign of Zodiac, which signifies ushering of the New Year.

Specially in Punjab, (the land of Green Revolution) and in the northern belt of India in general, farmers offer their prayers and rejoice. For, on this day, they commence reaping their harvest. The fields can be seen full of nature's bounty. Dressed in their typical folk attire, both men and women, enjoy the day with Bhangra and Gidda. Sweets are distributed, people embrace one another forgetting their differences. Everywhere there are people; giving vent to the joy; they feel in their hearts.

Baisakhi, however, has attained a new dimension as Guru Gobind Singh, on the very day of Baisakhi in 1669, had established the Khalsa Panth, and gave a final impetus to the course of the earlier nine Gurus of Sikhism.

A rural festival of North India, marking the beginning of the solar year (New year), Baisakhi is celebrated in Punjab with great fervour. For the Sikhs in particular the day is a combination of New Year and the commemoration of the founding of the Khalsa Panth (Sikh brotherhood). It also signifies the end of harvest of the main crop. During Baisakhi the farmers give thank to the Lord Almighty for their fortune and pray for a better crop in the coming year. Baisakhi witnesses a lot of socialising with friends, and relatives are invited and delicious meals are served.

On the day of Baisakhi, water is drawn from all the sacred rivers of India, and poured into the huge tank surrounding the Golden Temple.

JANMASHTAMI

The birth anniversary of Lord Krishna, the incarnation of Vishnu, is celebrated with great fervour all over India. Janmashtami in Mathura and Vrindavan, where Lord Krishna spent his childhood, witness a special spirit and enthusiasm. Temples and homes are beautifully decorated and lit. Nightlong prayers are offered and religious hymns are sung in temples. The priests chant holy mantras and bathe the idol with Panchamrit prepared by mixing Gangajal, milk, ghee (clarified butter), oil, and honey pouring it from a conch shell.

Janmashtami is celebrated in various parts of India to mark the birth of Lord Krishna. It is observed on the Ashtami day of the Bhadrapad (August-September) month, according to the Hindu calendar. The temples of Vrindavan witness an extravagant and colourful celebration on this occasion. Raslila is performed to present the events from the life of Krishna particularly to commemorate his love for Radha.

Lord Vishnu is invoked, in his human incarnation as Krishna on his birth anniversary, in the festival of Janmashtami. The idol of the infant Krishna is bathed at midnight and is placed in a cradle. Devotional songs and dances mark the celebration of this festive occasion all over Northern India.

On this day, in some parts of India, especially Maharashtra, youths celebrate it by breaking clay pots called 'Dahi-Handi', filled with curd and butter, suspended high above the ground. Young men and children form human pyramid to reach the pot and break it. This custom reminds the habit of Lord Krishna who used to steal butter in this manner from villagers along with his friends. The reason for this is that Gokul; the place where lord Krishna spent his childhood, used to produce a lot of milk and the people used to sell it in Mathura.

Rituals

On the day of Janamashtami, devotees keep daylong fast and keep themselves awake while chanting 'bhajans', until midnight. Midnight is the moment when Lord Krishna was born. The prayer ceremony is a simple affair. The priests chant holy mantras and bathe the idol of Lord Krishna, placed on a swing from a conch with 'charanamrit' or panchmarit prepared by mixing ganga-jal, milk, ghee (clarified butter), oil, and honey shell.

Midnight prayers amidst the sound of hymns and religious songs extol the greatness of Lord Krishna. Devotees break their day-long fast and chant - "Radhe Krishna, Hare Krishna, Radhe Radhe."

Celebrations

Mathura, the birthplace of Lord Krishna, where his parents lived in captivity of the evil Kansa, celebrates Janmashtami with great enthusiasm. Krishna as a young boy vanquished his maternal uncle Kansa to ascend the throne and free his parents.

In Vrindavan, every year the Raasleelas or the folk theatrical staging events of Krishna's life begin much before the Janmashtami day.

In Maharashtra, Janmashtami witnesses the exuberant enactment of the god's childhood endeavours to steal butter and curd from earthen pots beyond his reach. The earthen pots of curd and butter are hung up over the streets. Young men enacting an episode from Krishna's childhood form human pyramids by climbing on each other's shoulders and try to break these pots.

In South India, Janmashtami or Gokulashtami is celebrated with prayers, devotional renditions and offering of fruits and special prasadams to Lord Krishna. In some houses, a typical setting of 'Gokulam' is arranged with mud images of Devaki, Vasudeva with little Krishna perched in a basket on his head, as well as other things related to Krishna's legends.

RAM NAVMI

The birth of Lord Rama, the seventh incarnation of Lord Vishnu, in the Treta Yug is celebrated on the day of Ram Navmi. This day falls on the ninth day of the bright fortnight of the Hindu lunar month of Chaitra.

On this day, prayers are offered in the temples by devotees. As Lord Ram was born exactly at 12 O'clock at noon, the puja starts from the same time. On this day all the Hindus take early morning bath and then go to the nearest temple of Lord Ram to worship him.

Ayodhya, the birth place of Lord Ram, is the focus of great pomp and show in celebrations. A huge fair is organized for two days. 'Rathyatras' or 'chariot processions' of Ram, his wife Sita, brother Lakshman and Hanuman are taken out from many temples. At the Kanaka Bhawan Temple in Ayodhya, thousands of pilgrims converge and colourful processions are held. Shri Ram is said to have been born at mid day, when a priest formally announces his birth by placing a coconut in a cradle.

In some parts of India, especially Bihar, Haryana and Uttar Pradesh, public gatherings to hear sermon called Satsangs are organized to commemorate the birth of Rama. In Nagpur, Maharashtra, the Ram Janmostav Shobhayatra is celebrated with very high spirit at the Shri Poddareshwar Ram temple, which was built in 1923.

Many devotees stay awake on the previous night in many of the US Hindu temples, to commemorate the birth of Lord Ram next day. A havan is performed and they sing devotional songs in praise of Lord Ram and rock his image in cradles to celebrate his birth.

❑ ❑ ❑

B
NATIONAL FESTIVALS

REPUBLIC DAY (26TH JANUARY)

India became a republic on 26th January, 1950. It was on this day that the Constitution of India came into force. Since then the day is celebrated with great enthusiasm throughout the country.

The main celebrations are held in Delhi. The place which is the centre of attraction is the lawns from Vijaya Chowk to India Gate. Thousands of People from the capital and other cities and tourists from all over the world gather there to witness the procession. Those who can't come, watch it over the TV.

There is almost always one or the other foreign dignitary every year who is invited to attend the function. The President comes in a bullet-proof car from the Rashtrapati Bhawan and is received by the Prime Minister. The President hoists the flag and the National Anthem is sung by the school students.

The procession marks the endless variety of Indian culture and is symbolic of the progress made by India in various fields. Thus the military might of India is displayed not just by the military parade in which the three wings of the Indian forces participate but also by a display of various missiles, tanks and other weaponry possessed by the country. Contingents of NCC from schools and colleges drawn from all over the country follow the army personnel.

The main attraction to the spectators is the cultural pageants of different States and folk dances of the tribals. The school children also march and dance for a short distance.

The jets and helicopters blaze the sky and throw rose petals on the spectators and the processionists. Finally, gas balloons presenting the colours of the tricolour are released in the sky. Some of the important buildings like the Rashtrapati Bhawan, the Central Secretariat and the India Gate are tastefully illuminated at night. There is the beat of the retreat on 27th January when the tribals and others return to their home states.

INDEPENDENCE DAY (15ᵀᴴ AUGUST)

Independence Day is a national holiday. The day is celebrated all over India with great pomp and show.

India became independent on 15th August, 1947 after a long struggle. Jawaharlal Nehru who had spent the prime of his life in British jails while fighting against the mighty British empire, became the first Prime Minister of India and hoisted the Indian flag, tricolor, on the ramparts of the Red Fort in Delhi at 12:00 pm as the zero hour for 15th August started on this date in 1947. He called the moment India's "tryst with destiny".

Since then 15th August is celebrated every year as Independence Day. The main festival is held in Delhi. The Prime Minister of India hoists the tricolor early in the morning on the ramparts of the Red Fort before a mammoth gathering of Indian and foreign dignitaries, VIPs and common people. He makes a speech from behind a bullet proof glass cabin. In his speech, he explains the achievements and policies of the government and highlights the projects in hand. He lists the major problems of the country and how the government wants to address and harness them.

Small functions are held in all towns and cities and even in some big villages. In state capitals, the Chief Ministers and at other places Governors and other dignitaries such as Deputy Commissioners, senior police officers, Mayors of Municipal Corporation, etc. hoist the national flag. In schools and colleges the Presidents of Managing Committees or Principals of the institutions concerned do the ceremony. In all cases, the function always ends with the recitation of the National Anthem with due respect and regard.

GANDHI JAYANTI (2ᴺᴰ OCTOBER)

Mohandas Karamchand Gandhi widely known as Mahatma Gandhi, the apostle of peace and the Father of Nation, was born on 2nd October, 1869, at Porbandar in Gujarat. Gandhi Jayanti is celebrated as the birthday of Mahatma Gandhi. In his autobiography 'My Experiments With Truth,' Gandhi recalls that his childhood and teenage years were

☆☆ *Latest Essays & Letters* ☆☆

characterised by education in a local school. He married Kasturba at the age of 13.

At the age of eighteen, he went to England to study law. In 1891, Gandhi returned to India and started practice at Rajkot. In 1893, to plead a case of an Indian firm he went to South Africa. During his more than two decades of stay in South Africa, Gandhi protested against the discriminating treatment that was meted out to Indians. He protested against the Asiatic (Black) Act and the Transvaal Immigration Act by starting his non-violent Civil Disobedience Movement. Gandhiji returned to India in 1915. After an interrupted stay in Santiniketan in February-March, 1915, Gandhiji gathered his companions of Phoenix and established the Satyagraha Ashram in Ahmedabad city. This was shifted in June 1917 to the banks of the Sabarmati. This Ashram became platform for carrying out his social reforms, prime among which were Harijan welfare, rehabilitation of lepers and self-reliance through weaving Khadi.

Between 1917 and 1918, Gandhi participated in two peasant movements in Champaran (Bihar) and Kaira (Gujarat) besides the labour dispute in Ahmedabad itself.

For Gandhi 'non-violence' and truth were two inalienable virtues. He summed up the entire philosophy of his life as: "The only virtue I want to claim is truth and non-violence. I lay no claim to super human powers, I want none". The year 1926 was declared by Gandhi to be his year of silence. His famous march to Dandi in March 1930 started a countrywide movement to violate the Salt-Law. Gandhi was arrested on 4th May, 1930, and the Government struck hard to crush the movement, but failed. So Gandhi was set free on 26th January 1931; and following a pact between him and the British Viceroy, Lord Irwin (5th March 1931), he was prevailed upon to represent the Congress at the second Round Table Conference in London. In August 1932, providing for the introduction of separate electorate for the Depressed Classes, he opposed this attempt to divide the Hindu community and threatened to fast unto death to prevent it. But the situation was saved by the conclusion of the Poona Pact, which provided for special reservation of seats for the Depressed Classes in legislatures, but under joint electorate.

On 8th May 1933 he announced a fast for 21 days for the Harijan. After coming out of prison Gandhi devoted himself exclusively to the cause of the 'Harijans'. The weekly Harijan now took the place of the Young India, which had served the national cause from 1919 to 1932.

In 1942, his 'Quit India' slogan was to serve as the final signal to British dominion in India. The partition of India and Pakistan came as a personal shock to Gandhi. When the nation was rejoicing independence (1947), Gandhi went to Noakhali to ameliorate the conditions of the communal riot victims. On 30th January 1948, Gandhi was assassinated in New Delhi.

Mahatma Gandhi was a man of simple living and high thinking which reflects in Gandhi Jayanti with the festivities are sober and simple. A prayer meeting is held at Rajghat, Gandhi's samadhi in New Delhi. To mark the respect, that Gandhi had for all the religions and communities, representatives from different religions take part in it. Verses and prayers are read out from the holy books of all the religions. Gandhi's favourite song, 'Raghupati Raghava,' is invariably sung at all the meetings associated with the celebration of Gandhi Jayanti. Prayer meetings are held in various state capitals as well. Gandhi Jayanti is observed all over the country, both in government and non-government organisations.

TEACHER'S DAY (5ᵀᴴ SEPTEMBER)

Every year Teachers' Day is celebrated all over India on 5th September. It is because Dr. S. Radhakrishnan was born on this day.

Dr. S. Radhakrishnan who later became a great government dignitary, was earlier an outstanding teacher. He taught in India and later in England. He was greatly loved by his pupils for his scholarship and affable manners.

Teachers' day is celebrated in our school every year. On this day, teachers are given a break from their routine job of teaching. In their place, the students of XII class dress smartly as teachers and teach the junior classes for about an hour or so. All the students take them as real teachers for that period.

A day earlier, the school hall is tastefully decorated with colourful ribbons and bunting. The main function is held there. All the teachers are invited by the students through artistic invitation cards as their honoured guests and the most important persons.

A cultural programme especially prepared for the teachers is held. In this programme, skits, songs, dances, mimicry and parodies are presented by the students. The teachers are parodied in a light vein without giving any of them an occasion for being displeased.

The student representatives in their speeches praise the teachers for the good work they do as nation-builders. We pray for their prosperity and long life. We even offer apologies for any lapses on our part.

Then the teachers are presented beautiful bouquets and gifts, which usually create laughter without malice.

Last of all the teachers are invited to a light refreshment programme and we get blessings from them which they give liberally in tune with their general nature of love and generosity.

THE CHILDREN'S DAY (14ᵀᴴ NOVEMBER)

Pt. Jawahar Lal Nehru was a great lover of Children and on his birth day on November 14 is celebrated all over India as Children's Day. This was the day, long ago, in the year 1889, that Jawaharlal Nehru was born. Because children loved him so much, he was fondly called, 'Chacha Nehru'. Nehru had a soft corner for children and made it a point of spending a lot of time with them. He loved their innocence, vulnerability, honesty and non-pretenscious nature. Therefore, his birthday is celebrated as Children's Day.

Every school has its own way of celebrating this day. Be it a talk by the Principal at Assembly first thing in the morning followed by a cultural display of talent, entertaining the teachers, or a get together, and entertainment programme by the teachers for the children or a treat, whichever is feasible. But some sort of celebration normally takes place to single out this special day. In some schools, a video is shown on the life of Nehru.

Though several years have gone by, Nehru, still remains a symbol of love and affection in the hearts of the young.

❑ ❑ ❑

PHILANTHROPIC CHARACTER (PERSONALITIES)

GAUTAM BUDDHA

The childhood name of Gautama Buddha was Siddhartha. He was born in 563 BC. His father's name was Shuddhodhana who was the king of Kapilvastu. His mother's name was Maya Devi. She died when Gautama was only seven days old. It was his step-mother, Gautami Devi, who brought him up.

He grew up to be a very sensitive young man who was much concerned with the welfare of others. His father tried his best to keep him involved in the luxurious life of the palace. He did not want that young Siddhartha should go outside and see the misery of the world. But history tells us that the young man went out with his charioteer, Channa on three occasions, at least.

Siddhartha was greatly touched as he saw an old man, a sick man and a dead body. He wanted to do something to deliver the humanity from all such misery. He reflected on this problem for long. At last on hearing some words from the mouth of a hermit which encouraged him to renounce the world, he decided to leave the palace and go into the forest for meditation. Before going, he had a lasting glance on his beloved wife Yashodhra and son, Rahul, who were enjoying a sound sleep at midnight.

He started austere meditation to know the secret of life and death and observed long fasts. At last, he got enlightenment under the Bodhi tree at Gaya. Now, he became the 'Buddha' the enlightened one.

He delivered his first sermon at Sarnath. At first, five persons became his disciples. Soon, his message began to spread far and wide and the number of his disciples grew quickly. Buddhist 'maths' were later established all over the country.

He was an agnostic. He challenged the truth of the Vedas. He laid stress on truth and reason. He preached that the sole cause of misery was our desires which should be controlled to get peace and happiness. He laid emphasis on the middle path and exhorted his disciples to follow the eight fold path to get rid of misery. In essence, his message means service to mankind and all living beings without any selfish motives.

MAHATMA ISHA (JESUS CHRIST)

In the olden times Jewish priests were very wicked. Their holy book said that people should hate their enemies. At that time a brilliant child was born on December 25, B.C. 4 in the family of a carpenter in the village Nazreth. His mother's name was Mary. When he was twelve year old his knowledge about God was more than the priests. At the age of twenty, he went in a jungle and kept fast for forty days and discovered the true path of life.

He returned home and began to teach people that one should shed hatred and love their enemies. The most important lesson he taught to the people of the village was "Do to others only those things you would like them to do to you."

He told the people that the world had grown wicked-But God is kind enough to forgive everyone who felt sorry for his mistakes and confess them. He became very famous and thousands of people flocked to listen to him from far off places.

The priests of the Jews feared to lose their power so they began to hate Jesus and even started planning to kill him. On their complaint Roman Governor told them that he had no reason to arrest him. The Jewish priests conspired and bribed Jesus's friend Judas to capture him. After capturing Jesus, they produced him before Governor, he didn't find any fault with Jesus. The Governor was compelled to order for his crucifixion as Jesus said nothing in his self defence.

Thus the lighting figure sacrificed his life for the sins of mankind.

On 25th December Christians all over the world celebrate the birth or Nativity of Jesus Christ, the founder of Christianity.

Guru Nanak Dev Ji

A precious child was born in 1469 in khatri family at Talwandi, near Lahore. The village is called Nankana Sahib which is now in Pakistan. The name of the boy was Nanak, known to the world as Guru Nanak Dev. At the age of seven he joined the village school. He was very intelligent, and learned the alphabet in one day. Once he composed a beautiful hymn which is now in Guru Granth Sahib.

He used to think about God for hours together. When his father gave him twenty rupees to do some profitable business, he spent the money on feeding the hungry men. Nanak was married at the age of fourteen, But even marriage could not stop him from thinking about God. His father sent him to Sultanpur and was made a Government store-keeper by the Governor, Daulat Khan Lodhi. He was quite sincere to his work. One morning after taking a bath in Kalibai river, he went into the forest. There he heard the command of God to teach the people to remember Him. He turned saint from that day.

He preached that the people are not Hindus and Muslims but the children of one God. He believed in one God.To spread his message he visited many places in India. He taught people to believe in God. His mission became popular and he soon had a large following. He went to Arabia also. After his return from there he lived near river Tapi at Kartarpur until he died.

Swami Vivekananda

Swami Vivekananda is one of the great luminaries who have done India proud. He was greatly influenced by his parents who were a deeply religious couple.

His real name was Narendranath Dutt. He was born on 9th January, 1862 in Calcutta.

Even as a child he was very fond of meditating. He had deep spiritual experiences even at this tender age.

The most important change in his life came in 1881 when he met Shri Ramakrishna Paramahansa.

The most important question that he asked Ramakrishna was : "How do you see God?" Even more impressive was the answer : "I see God as I see you."

The young Narendranath was so impressed that he at once accepted Ramakrishna as his spiritual teacher.

Throughout his life, Narendranath loved this meeting in his mind and went out to serve humanity all over the world as his mission, realizing the spirit of God persuading the heart of every human being.

He genuinely loved India as the great country which could impart spiritual knowledge to the whole world. He expressed powerfully the Indian spiritual viewpoint at the Parliament of Religions in Chicago in 1893 and was hailed as a great scholar and spiritualist all over the world. The most important point is that he did India proud as never before.

He travelled far and wide and gave lectures conveying the message of his teacher and the ancient spiritual heritage of India.

He is a symbol of courage and loyalty to the nation, particularly with the youth, whom he loved very much.

It was after his death he came to be known as Swami Vivekananda. He passed away on July 4, 1902. The Ramakrishna Mission which he established is still doing yeoman's service to people.

MOTHER TERESA

Agnes Gonxha Bejaxhiu was born in August 1910 at Skopje in Yugoslavia. In 1928 she went to Ireland. There she entered the Loreto congregation. At that time in Bengal the sisters of Loreto were carrying out missionary work. A year later she sailed to India with a longing to join them. She became the Principal of St. Agnes' High School for Girls at Calcutta (now Kolkata) after years of teaching in the congregation's schools and convents.

A large slum near the school caught her attention. She was deeply moved by the condition of the lowly creatures. Their sufferings stirred her inner self to give up her comfortable living. Led by her call within she went out into the cruel and merciless metropolis. After she took Indian citizenship in 1948 she went about collecting human wrecks on the streets, housed them and begged from door to door for food.

She founded the Missionaries of Charity in 1950 with just a few sisters. In 1956, she founded the 'Nirmal Hriday', a home for the dying destitutes in the house donated by the Calcutta corporation authorities. Help from the people was little. She did not give up. The hostility of the local people who wanted to drive her out changed when she housed a dying priest stricken by cholera whom no one would touch.

After Nirmal Hriday homes for destitute children, leper colonies and clinics for the poorest followed. In 1963 she founded the missionary Brothers of Charity. Today, they run hundreds of homes in Asia, Europe, America and Australia. She became renowned world over as Mother Teresa—the living saint.

She won many awards and honours. She won the Nobel Peace Prize in 1979 and Bharat Ratna in 1980. In 1990 she was conferred the Soviet Land Nehru Award for promoting friendship among the people and helping the poor and unfortunate. She had received the honour as 'Angel of Peace'. The awards and admiration had not changed her life or her sisters. She had devoted her life to the service of mankind.

Mother Teresa had also led various peace missions. She began with a fervent desire to do for others and ended her life long service by setting up institutions for the helpless, handicapped, orphans and leprosy-inflicted victims. She did not like to talk about herself and felt at peace among the people of her homes. She began her day with an early morning mass and visited all her homes wherever she happened to be. She enjoyed her work and inspired many to join her.

In 1991 she suffered pneumonia, leading to congestive heart failure. Before she died in September 1997 due to cardiac arrest she stepped down as the head of her order. Her death stunned millions of people all over the world. She was given a state funeral and was laid to rest at Mother House in Calcutta.

ISHWAR CHANDRA VIDYASAGAR

Pandit Ishwar Chandra Vidyasagar, a Sanskrit pandit, was an educator, reformer, writer, and a philanthropist. He was considered to be one of the greatest intellectuals and activists of the nineteenth century.

Ishwar Chandra Vidyasagar was born in a Brahmin family at Birsingha in Midnapore district. His parents, though poor, managed to send him to Calcutta (now Kolkata) for studies after he finished his early education at the village *pathshala*. Ishwar studied at the Sanskrit College, Calcutta (now Kolkata) from 1829 to 1841. He bagged all the prizes and scholarships for the best performance. Evaluating his performance in various courses - poetry, rhetoric, Vendanta, *Smrti*, astrology and logic, the College Committee endowed Ishwar Chandra with the title of *Vidyasagar* (sea of knowledge) in 1839.

At the age of 21, Ishwar Chandra Vidyasagar started his career as the head pandit of the Fort William College, Calcutta (now Kolkata). He joined the Sanskrit College as a professor in 1850. In the following year, he became the principal of the college. Concurrently, with his Sanskrit College position, the government entrusted him in 1855 with the added responsibility of the Special Inspector of Schools for the districts of Hooghli, Burdwan, Midnapore and Nadia.

As Special Inspector of Schools, Vidyasagar used his position to encourage landholders and other solvent people to establish educational institutions. Within his inspection zone, he was instrumental in founding dozens of schools, several of which were for girls. Some schools were established at his own initiative and with his financial support.

He was also an honorary office bearer of several organisations including Asiatic Society and Bethune Society. In 1858, he was made one of the first fellows of the Calcutta University. Ishwar received a certificate of Honour at the Imperial Assemblage in January 1877 and in January 1880, was made a CIE. He also received honours and felicitations from many social, cultural and scientific organisations.

Vidyasagar was a great reformer and thinker. His reforming mind has found most concrete expression in his socio-religious thoughts. He raised questions about early marriage, polygamy, widow remarriage, and many other ills stifling social developments.

The enactment of the Act of 1856, legalising widow remarriage and the Civil Marriage Act of 1872, restricting bigamy and child marriage and encouraging widow remarriage, owed a great deal to Vidyasagar, whose writings and activities had helped to create public opinion in favour of these issues.

Vidyasagar's monumental contribution to educational institution building was his Calcutta Metropolitan Institution, a model college with attached schools, which he established in 1864 at his own cost.

His stature as an educator, reformer, writer and philanthropist grew to such a height that, at his death on July 29, 1891, the whole nation, irrespective of race, religion and caste, mourned. The newspapers and magazines published obituaries and features applauding his deeds and achievements; poets and writers, including Rabindranath Tagore, wrote poems and features in his memory. In these remembrances and recollections, Vidyasagar was rated as the greatest man of the century. The evaluation remains unchanged even today.

❑ ❑ ❑

THE MAN OF LETTERS/LITER-ARY/SPORTS PERSONALITIES

TULSIDAS

Among the great saints of India, Tulsidas's name comes among the foremost in mind.

He was born in 1540 at Banda in Uttar Pradesh. If Mirabai and Surdas are known for their great love for Lord Krishna, Tulsidas is known for his undying devotion for Lord Rama.

It is said that on the birth of Tulsidas, the astrologers told his parents that the child was likely to bring great misfortune to them. They were so scared that they discarded him.

As chance would have it, Tulsidas actually lost his parents when he was just five.

Being penniless, he had to work hard in fields to make a bare living. He had even to beg. It is said that he was considered a Jonah or highly unlucky creature even by beggars and they would not allow him to beg with them or sit near them.

A real change came in his life when he had a meeting with Guru Nar Hari Das. The latter instilled into his mind the idea of worshipping Lord Rama which all his followers were bidden to do.

As he grew up, he was married to a beautiful girl, Ratnavali.

He was so much enamoured of her that he forgot even Lord Rama whom he had vowed to worship.

In an angry tone, Ratnavali said to him, "Had you worshipped Rama even with half of the devotion you have for me, you would have realized Him by now."

These words had a lasting effect on Tulsidas. He started praying to and worshipping Rama with full concentration of mind.

In course of time, he wrote several books, such as Ramcharitmanas, Geetavali, Kavitavali, Vinayapatrika, etc.

His most famous work which he completed in 1600 is Ramcharitmanas which is still read with utmost devotion in every home in India by the people who love Lord Rama.

He died in 1632 at Kashi. Tulsidas is an immortal saint of India who has had an undying impact on Indian religious belief.

MIRABAI

India has given birth to soldiers as well as saints. Among the saints of India, Mirabai holds a very high place.

She is still remembered all over India for her sweet, highly devotional hymns and bhajans.

She was born in a royal family in 1499. Even as a child, she got obsessed with her love for Lord Krishna.

She considered only Lord Krishna as her husband. Even when she was married to the Rana of Mewar, she did not stop loving and worshipping Lord Krishna whom she regarded as true and real husband.

She regularly sang hymns and danced before the idol of Lord Krishna in temples and loved to live in company of saints.

She became very popular with the people in Mewar and the adjoining areas. They also began to sing and dance in front of idol of Krishna alongwith her.

On the other hand, the royal family of Mewar got enraged with her for her such unworldly religious activities.

They at first tried to dissuade her from these activities. Having failed in these efforts, the Rana of Mewar sent her a cup of poison. She drank it up readily. Miraculously, the poison had no ill effect on her.

Mirabai's life became a saga of hardship and misery. But she remained undaunted. In that age of medieval period, when women were under the thumb of their husbands, inlaws and other men, she remained undaunted even when she was turned out of the palace. As a redoultable woman, refusing to bow before male domination, she deserves to be hailed as the first feminist of the world.

She died in 1547. It is said that she merged herself into the idol of Lord Krishna.

MUNSHI PREMCHAND

Munshi Premchand was one of the greatest literary figures of modern Hindi literature. His stories vividly portray the social scenario of those times. Premchand wrote on the realistic issues of the day-communalism, corruption, zamindari, debt, poverty, colonialism, etc. He avoided the use of highly Sanskritised Hindi and instead used the dialect of the common people.

Premchand's real name was Dhanpat Rai Srivastava. He was born on July 31, 1880 in Lamahi near Varanasi where his father, Munshi Ajaayab Lal was a clerk in the post office. Premchand lost his mother when he was just seven years old. His father married again. Premchand was very close to his elder sister. His early education was in a *madarasa* under a *Maulavi*, where he learnt Urdu. When he was studying in the ninth class he was married, much against his wishes. He was only fifteen years old at that time.

Premchand lost his father, when he was sixteen years old. Premchand was left responsible for his stepmother and stepsiblings. He earned five rupees a month tutoring a lawyer's child. Premchand passed his matriculation exam with great effort and took up a teaching position, with a monthly salary of eighteen rupees. While working, he studied privately and passed his Intermediate and BA examinations. Later, Premchand worked as the deputy sub-inspector of schools in what was then the United Provinces.

In 1910, he was hauled up by the District Magistrate in Jamirpur for his anthology of short stories, *Soz-e-Watan* (Dirge of the Nation), which was labelled seditious. His book, *Soz-e-Watan* was banned by the then British government, which burnt all of its copies. Initially, Premchand wrote in Urdu under the name of 'Nawabrai'. However, when his novel, *Soz-e-Watan* was confiscated by the British, he started writing under the pseudonym, 'Premchand'.

Before Premchand, Hindi literature consisted mainly of fantasy or religious works. He brought realism to Hindi literature. He wrote over 300 stories, a dozen novels and two plays. The stories have been compiled and published as *Maansarovar*. His famous creations are: *Panch Parameshvar, Idgah, Shatranj Ke Khiladi, Poos Ki Raat, Bade Ghar Ki Beti, Kafan, Udhar Ki Ghadi, Namak Ka Daroga, Gaban, Godaan, Sevasadan, Rangbhumi, Kayakalp* and *Nirmala*.

Premchand was a great social reformer. He married a child widow named Shivarani Devi. She wrote a book on him, *Premchand Gharmein* after his death. In 1921, he answered Gandhiji's call and resigned from his job. He worked to generate patriotism and nationalistic sentiments in the general populace. When the editor of the journal, *Maryaada* was jailed in the freedom movement, Premchand worked for a time as the editor of that journal. Afterwards, he worked as the Principal in a school in the Kashi Vidyapeeth.

The main characteristic of Premchand's writings is his interesting storytelling and use of simple language. His writings have been translated not only into all Indian languages, but also Russian, Chinese, and many other foreign languages.

Besides being a great novelist, Premchand was also a social reformer and thinker. His greatness lies in the fact that his writings embody social purpose and social criticism rather than mere entertainment. Literature according to him is a powerful means of educating public opinion. He believed in social evolution and his ideal was equal opportunities for all. Premchand died in 1936 and has since been studied both in India and abroad as one of the greatest writers of the century.

RABINDRA NATH TAGORE

Rabindra Nath Tagore was born on 8th May, 1861 in Jorasanku in Kolkata. His father, Maharishi Debendra Nath was a great landlord and was known as 'Thakur', the word which got changed into 'Tagore'. His mother's name was Sharda Devi. He was the youngest of the fourteen children in the family of Debendra Nath and Sharda Devi.

☆☆ *Latest Essays & Letters* ☆☆

Rabindra Nath Tagore was one of the greatest men of India and he was easily one of the greatest literary personages of the world. He was a versatile genius, being a poet, novelist, playwright, essayist , short story writer, statesman, musician, painter, philosopher, actor, educationist and freedom fighter all rolled into one. He was both a great nationalist and an internationalist and universalist and humanist in equal measure.

He wrote originally in Bengali but later translated his own works into English. His world famous work of lyrics, the Gitanjali, for which he won the Nobel Prize in 1913, was also originally written in Bengali but later translated into English by the poet himself.

He was a great lover of his country, of humanity and children in particular. He believed in non-violence and rejected traditionalism as much as western chauvinism. The Indian National Anthem *'Jana Gana Mana'* was written by him. He also set up the Shantiniketan with the money he got from the Nobel Prize. He gave up the title of 'Sir' as a protest against the Jallianwala Bagh tragedy in 1919. He died on 8th August, 1941.

SACHIN TENDULKAR : THE GREATEST BATSMAN IN THE WORLD

Sachin Tendulkar bade adieu to cricket on November 16, 2013 after remaining the stem of the foundation of Indian Cricket. He played his 200th and the last test match against West Indies at Wankhede Stadium of Mumbai. The government of India has honoured him with the 'Bharat Ratna', the highest citizen honour of India. The master-blaster, in his career of 24 years in cricket, has set many records to his credit.

This youngest son of a simple Marathi professor used to hold his bat in his hand and weave dreams of his future. His luck favoured him for the first time when Ramakant Achrekar, known as the Dronacharya of the cricket world, accepted, him as his disciple. The assayer eyes of Achrekar had visualised that this student (called Sachin) had come to learn from him from the core of his heart. The teacher had realised that one day, the bat of this student would sing such times as would make the cricket lovers of the world gyrate for long periods. Sachin also toiled hard along with Achrekar and at the age of thirteen, he created history in partnership with his childhood friend, Vinod Kambli. Both of these players made a record partnership of 664 runs for the sixth wicket in school's cricket competition. This was the first ever success of Sachin's life, which acted like a tonic for him. After this his hunger for such achievements continued to grow.

Sachin had to wait for nearly five years to score the first century in one-day cricket matches. However, after scoring the first century, he liked the century scoring innings so much that he became engrossed in the efforts to score a century in every innings he played. The idea of Sachin's growing hunger can be made through the fact that in 1994, Sachin, who had scored a century in seventy-ninth one-day match against Australia (in Colombo), had scored 49 centuries till December 23, 2012 when he bade adieu to it. In his career of 24 years, Sachin has scored 18,426 runs in one-day games (with 49 centuries) and 15,921 runs (with 51 centuries) in Test matches.

On 16 March, 2012 while playing in Asia Cup at Mirpur in Bangladesh against Bangladesh, Sachin completed his 100th century. The century of centuries has been completed in the history of cricket for the first-time. This was Sachin's 49th century in the one-day matches. He has scored 51 centuries in test-cricket. Sachin has scored centuries against all the nations in the international cricket. The president while appreciating his contribution in the game has nominated him to Rajya Sabha. In the history of last sixty years, Sachin is the only sportsperson to be nominated for the Upper House.

VIRAT KOHLI : THE CRICKET CHAMP

Virat Kohli is an Indian International cricketer. He is the captain of the Indian cricket team in all three formats.

Virat Kohli was born on 5 November, 1988 in Delhi to Prem and Saroj Kohli. Virat attended Vishal Bharti and Savier Convent School. His father worked as a lawyer and untimely died in December 2006. He has an elder brother and a sister.

Virat first came into the spotlight when he played for Delhi in a Ranji trophy match against Karnataka on the day of his father's death. His team mates needed him at a crucial moment when he was much more needed at home. He preferred to do his duty and scored 90 runs. That was an act of great commitment to the team and his innings turned out to be crucial.

Virat has been the recipient of many awards such as the Sir Garfield Sobers Trophy (ICC Cricketer of the Year) in 2017 and 2018; ICC Test Player of the Year 2018; ICC ODI Player of the Year in 2012, 2017 and 2018 and Wisden Leading Cricketer in the World in 2016, 2017. He was given the Arjuna Award in 2013, the Padma Shri under the sports category in 2017 and the Rajiv Gandhi Khel Ratna, the highest sporting honour in India, in 2018. He is ranked as one of the world's most famous athletes by ESPN and one of the most valuable athlete brands by Forbes. In 2018, Time magazine named Kohli one of the 100 most influential people in the world.

A stand at Arun Jaitley Stadium is named Virat Kohli Stand on 12 September 2019.

MC MARY KOM : QUEEN OF THE RING

MC Mary Kom is an Indian boxer. The full name of Mary Kom is Mangte Chungneijang Mary Kom. She has been given the title 'Queen of the Ring'. Mary Kom was born in Kangathei, Manipur, India on 1 March 1983. Her parents are Mangte Tonpa Kom and Mangte Akham Kom. Her husband is K Onler Kom. She is mother of three children.

She started boxing in the international level only at the age of 18. She won 5 gold medals and one silver medal in Women's World Amateur Boxing Championships. She had to gain weight for the Olympics as there were only three categories. At 2012 Olympic she competed under 51 kg category and won bronze medal. At an interview she apologised to the people for not winning gold medal.

For her tremendous performance she has won many awards and accolades. She won Arjuna Award, Padma Shree, Padma Bhushan and Rajiv Gandhi Khel Ratna Awards in 2003, 2006, 2013 and 2009. She is also called "Magnificent Mary" for her performance.

Her interest in boxing was inspired by the success of Manipuri male boxer Dingko Singh. She took to sports in an effort to provide some financial support to her family. She had established herself as a boxer par excellence when she won a Silver medal at the 2008 Asian Women's Boxing Championship in India and a fourth successive Gold medal at the AIBA Women's World Boxing Championship in China, which was followed by a Gold medal at the 2009 Asian Indoor Games in Vietnam. Next year, in the 2010 Asian Women Boxing Championship in Kazakhstan, she again won a Gold medal, a feat which she repeated at the AIBA Women's World Boxing Championship in Barbados which was her fifth Gold medal at this Championship. In the 2010 Asian Games, she won a Bronze medal. In 2011, she won a Gold medal in the 48 kg class at the Asian Women's Cup in China and won a Gold medal again in the 51 kg class at the Asian Women's Boxing Championship in Mongolia. She won a gold medal in Incheon Asian Games–2014 in women's flyweight category (48-51 kg). She is the first Indian woman boxer to win a gold medal in Asian Games. She has been chosen as the most valuable player of India's Incheon Asian Games Campaign. Impressed by the resilience of her spirit and her never-say-die approach, the eminent film-maker, Sanjay Leela Bhansali has made a biopic "Mary Kom" where the world-famous beauty-turned actor Priyanka Chopra portrays Mary Kom's powerful character.

On 26 April 2016, Kom was nominated by the President of India as a member of the Rajya Sabha, the upper house of the Indian Parliament. In March 2017, the Ministry of Youth Affairs and Sports, Government of India, appointed Mary Kom along with Akhil Kumar as national observers for boxing. On 8 November 2017, she clinched an unprecedented fifth gold medal (48 kg) at the ASBC Asian Confederation women's boxing championships held at Ho Chi Minh in Vietnam.

On 24 November 2018, she created history by becoming the first woman to win 6 World Championships, achieving this feat at the 10th AIBA Women's World Boxing Championships held in New Delhi.

❑ ❑ ❑

NATIONAL LEADER OR NATION BUILDER

NARENDRA MODI

Mr. Narendra Modi is the present Prime Minister of India. He was born into a poor family on September 17, 1950 in Vadnagar in Mehsana district of the erstwhile Bombay Presidency. He is the third of the six children born to a small teaseller, Damodardas Mulchand Modi and Heeraben.

During his childhood, he assisted his father in earning bread by holding a kettle of tea in hand and even sold drinking water at the railway station. After completing his schooling from Vadnagar, he joined Gujarat University and became a pracharak in the Rashtriya Swayamsevak Sangh (RSS).

When Mr. Keshubhai Patel became the Chief Minister of Gujarat, Modi was made General Secretary of the Bharatiya Janata Party (BJP). After the stepping down of Mr. Keshubhai Patel as the Chief Minister of Gujarat, he was chosen for the post by the BJP on October 7, 2001.

His administrative acumen, clear vision and personal integrity helped him register a landslide victory in the Assembly elections held in Gujarat in December 2002, 2007 and 2012 and become the Chief Minister for three consecutive terms.

He became the Prime Minister of India twice in 2014 and 2019 after winning with full majority in Loksabha elections. He is the live example of the fact that even a poor humble man can touch unimaginable heights by dint of his determination and hard work.

Narendra Modi on February 22, 2019 received the prestigious Seoul Peace Prize 2018 for his contribution to international cooperation and fostering global economic growth. In October 2018, he received UN's highest environmental award, the Champions of the Earth. He also received the Order of St. Andrew, the highest civilian honour of Russia on April 12, 2019.

NETAJI SUBHASH CHANDRA BOSE

Subhash Chandra Bose was one of the greatest freedom fighters of India. He was born on January 23,1897 at Cuttack in Odisha. His father, Janakinath Bose was a renowned lawyer of the area. His mother, Prabhavati Devi was a highly learned and religious-minded lady.

Subhash Chandra imbibed many of his religious views from her. Some other persons who influenced him greatly were his teacher Beni Madhab Das, C.R. Das and Swami Vivekananda.

He was a very intelligent, precocious, patriotic child with revolutionary ideas in his mind from the very beginning. He did his graduation from the former Presidency College (now it is Presidency University) in 1919. Later, he appeared and passed the ICS examination only to please his father. But actually his heart was framed for serving his motherland and getting it liberated from the foreign rule. In politics, his real mentors were Lokmanya Tilak and Sri Aurobindo Ghose more than Gandhi. Hence he was not much attracted towards the Non-Cooperation Movement which was started by Gandhiji in the 1920's.

In Bengal, the National Movement was being spearheaded by C.R. Das and Subhash Chandra was especially attracted towards him. The young Subhash arranged demonstration in Kolkata and was put behind the bars. Later, he had to be released. He was appointed the Chief Executive Officer of the Calcutta Corporation. Earlier in 1924, he had been arrested under the special ordinance and was sent to Mandalay.

He was elected President of the Congress at the 1938 Haripura Session. Thereafter, he formed the Forward Bloc. Actually, he was in favour of fixing a deadline for freedom and giving an ultimatum to the British government to leave India. He led the Indian National Army. On July 2, 1943, he gave the famous slogan *"Delhi Chalo"*. His words, "Give me your blood and I will give you freedom" can never be forgotten by his countrymen.

He went in disguise as a Pathan first to Germany and then managed to reach Japan. The radio Tokyo declared that Netaji died in an air crash in 1945. His death is still a matter of controversy for some people.

MAHATMA GANDHI

Mohandas Karamchand Gandhi, whom people lovingly called 'Bapu' is popularly known as Mahatma Gandhi. He was born on October 2, 1869 at porbandar in Gujarat. He received his early education at home and was highly influenced by his parents. He was sent to England for higher studies. He studied law and in 1891 was called to the Bar. He returned to India and set up his legal practice but could not succeed as a lawyer.

Two years later he went to South Africa for a legal case. He guided the Indians there to struggle against injustice and tyranny which they were suffering under cruel laws. It was a non-violent successful movement.

After 21 years he returned to India and joined the struggle for India's Independence. Sabarmati was the centre of his many activities of non-violent, non-cooperation movements. For this, he was sent to jail many times. He fought against injustice fearlessly and was a tyranny everywhere. He strongly believed in Satyagraha which is a fight based on truth against injustice, cruelty and untruth. He successfully led the countrymen to their freedom in August 1947.

Mahatma Gandhi was a great humanitarian. He was a God fearing and spiritual minded person. The Father of the Nation not only served the country but worked throughout his life for the upliftment of the weaker sections of the society and the removal of many social and the moral evils.

He lived a splendid long life and has set great moral standards before us. He showed to the world the true way to peace. He wished to see India prosper but he became a martyr for the noble cause of Hindu-Muslim unity at the time of partition when a religious fanatic, Nathuram Godse, shot him dead on January 30, 1948. His last words were 'Hey Ram'.

SARDAR VALLABHBHAI PATEL

The full name of Sardar Patel was Vallabhbhai Patel. The title 'Sardar' was given to him by Mahatma Gandhi.

Sardar Patel was one of the most illustrious sons of India. He was one of the greatest freedom fighters of our country.

After Independence, he became the Deputy Prime Minister of India. He is generally called, the "Iron Man of India". It is mainly because of his strong will and firm determination in the service of his motherland.

He was born in Karamsad village in Gujarat on October, 21, 1875. The name of his father was Jhaver Bhai Patel who was a brave, patriotic man, having fought in the army of Rani Lakshmi Bai of Jhansi against the British in 1857.

Sardar Patel got his early education in his village. Later, he went to Nadiad and then to Baroda to get higher education.

His father was a poor peasant. Still, Sardar Patel somehow saved money and went to England where he studied law and became a barrister.

He was greatly influenced by Gandhiji and he jumped into politics in 1918. His first important achievement was the removal of the system of "Begar'" from Gujarat.

Another of his achievement was his being successful in getting the grievances of the peasants redressed regarding payments of revenue even on the failure of their crops. This he got done through the Gandhian non-violent methods.

One of the greatest moments of his success came in regard to the Bardoli Satyagrah. It was his success that earned him the title "Sardar' from Gandhiji.

One of his greatest fortes was his ability to organize and manage. This was lucidly clear in all the campaigns he undertook.

He took an active part in the Quit India Movement in 1942. He went to jail several times in his life.

When India became free, he held the portfolio of the Home Minister alongwith being the Deputy Prime Minister. He had already held several positions before India became free.

After Independence, his great achievement was the merger of more than six hundred princely states into the Indian Union. His police action in the erstwhile Hyderabad speaks volumes of his grit and statesmanship.

SARDAR BHAGAT SINGH

Bhagat Singh is one of the greatest martyrs that India has produced. He is the icon and model of young people in particular.

He was born on November 11, 1907 at Banga village in the district of Lyalpur (now Faisalabad) in Pakistan. His father, Kishan Singh, and uncle Ajit Singh, both were revolutionaries and were released from jail on the day he was born.

He was a very brilliant student at school. While studying at DAV School in Lahore, young Bhagat Singh came into contact with some well-known political leaders like Lala Lajpat Rai and Rash Bihari Bose. The famous revolutionary Kartar Singh Sarabha was his model. Even as a child he was greatly moved by the Jallianwalah Bagh massacre. He expressed his desire to grow guns in the Indian soil to force the British rulers to quit India.

In 1928, he attended a meeting of revolutionaries in Delhi and came into contact with Chandrasekhar Azad. The two formed the "Hindustan Samajvadi Prajatantra Sangha."

He learnt about the brutal death of Lala Lajpat Rai at the hands of a British police officer in 1928 while leading a peaceful but noisy demonstration against the Simon Commission. In order to avenge the murder of Lajpat Rai, he killed Saunders. He alongwith his companions, Rajguru and Sukhdev, was hanged on 23rd March, 1931 on the bank of Ravi near Ferozepur. Earlier, he had floated Naujawan Bharat Sabha and also thrown a bomb in the Assembly with Batukeshwar Dutt.

He wanted a free, secular, happy prosperous India. Indians can never forget his sacrifice for the motherland.

BAL GANGADHAR TILAK

Bal Gangadhar Tilak was born on 23rd July, 1856 at Ratnagiri. He belonged to the ruling sect of the Maratha Kingdom on the Chitpavan Brahmins. This sect was a class of strictly orthodox Brahmins.

His father was an ordinary school teacher who later rose to be the inspector of schools. Bal Gangadhar passed his matriculation examination at the age of sixteen and was married soon after, but meanwhile he lost his father. He pursued his higher education at Deccan College, Pune and did his graduation in 1877.

He was not interested in joining any service. He wanted to serve the people in the real sense. Alongwith two of his friends, Agarkar and Chiplunkar, he started the New English School at Pune. He also started two weeklies in 1881 - *Maratha* and *Kesari*. The former was in English and the latter in Marathi. In 1885, the Deccan Education Society was established mainly because of his efforts.

He was a great lover of the great Indian heritage and a keen admirer of Shivaji. In order to enhance the spirit of patriotism and cooperation among the Indian people, he re-organised the Ganapati and the Shivaji festivals.

He opposed tooth and nail the partition of Bengal in 1905. He was arrested and sent to Mandalay in Burma (now Myanmar) to serve a six year term. He utilized his time in prison in scholarly pursuits and wrote *'Gita Rahasya'*, a commentary on the Gita. After returning from jail, he started the Home Rule Movement. He was one of the delegates of the Home Rule League that visited England in 1918. He breathed his last on August 1, 1920.

He will always be remembered for his words: "Swaraj is my birth right and I shall have it." He was one of the greatest Indian leaders who roused the masses against the foreign rule and imbued them with the spirit of patriotism, social service and sacrifice. He has left an indelible impression on the history of India.

GOPAL KRISHNA GOKHALE

Gopal Krishna Gokhale was one of the greatest freedom fighters of India. He belonged to the moderate group among the freedom fighters. He did not believe in confrontation and violence.

He was born on 9th March, 1866. He was greatly influenced by his mother.

After finishing his schooling in 1881, he joined the Bombay University for higher studies. He graduated from this university in 1884.

☆☆ *Latest Essays & Letters* ☆☆

Thereafter, he joined the Fergusson College, Poona. He was a brilliant student and an efficient teacher. He rose to be the Principal of this college.

Gokhale was known for his magical memory. It is said that he often taught his classes all the English literature, particularly poetry, from memory, as he had learnt and that perhaps effortlessly, most of the poems prescribed in syllabus to various classes, by heart.

His good memory, knowledge and command over language also enabled him to become a great orator and after becoming a brilliant follower of justice Ranade, the great thinker, his own reputation as a great Indian also got augmented manifold.

Surprisingly, Gandhiji who himself was later to impress so many Indian leaders and people himself came under the influence of Gokhale whom he regarded as his mentor. It was mainly because of his wisdom, political acumen, straightforwardness and, above all, truthfulness. In the eyes of Gandhiji, Gokhale was the model of a perfect man.

Gokhale was elected the president of the Congress in 1905. He started the "Servants of India Society." His aim was to channelise the energies of the young people towards social and public service.

No doubt, he wanted freedom for India, yet quite reasonably, he wanted to give the devil his due, and for this reason he had words of praise for the British rule.

He believed in the dictum "Work is worship". Overwork told upon his health and he breathed his last on February 19, 1915. No doubt, he was a patriot through and through and is so remembered to this day.

RAJA RAM MOHAN ROY

Raja Ram Mohan Roy is known as a great social reformer who tried to improve the lot of the poor, particularly women.

He was born in a Brahmin family in Bengal on 22nd May, 1772. He was a great scholar and linguist. He had a thorough study of the Hindu as well as Muslim scriptures.

He knew several languages such as Bangla, English, Urdu, Sanskrit, Persian, French, Latin, Arabic, etc. He was in favour of English being introduced in India. He believed that the knowledge of English could bring awakening among the Indian masses and they would automatically demand and work for freedom. Moreover, the knowledge of English could be helpful in getting a job.

It was one of the Mughal Emperors who gave the title of Raja to him for the services done to him. He also served in the East India Company from 1805 to 1815.

After his retirement from the East India Company, he spent most of his time in serving the Indian people.

He was very eager to bring about reforms in all spheres of the Indian society such as social, economic, religious, political and educational. He wanted to change the life-style of Indians and raise their living standard.

In particular, he was the champion of women's, cause. In course of time, his voice became so powerful that he persuaded and partly forced Lord William Bentinck, the then Governor General of India, to declare *Sati* an illegal institution in 1928. Thus, he was one of the potent pioneers who got Sati banned.

He founded the Brahmo Samaj to preach against idol worship. He breathed his last in 1833. He will always be remembered as a great Indian.

LAL BAHADUR SHASTRI

Lal Bahadur Shastri could serve as the Prime Minister of India only for a short period, about one and a half year to be precise, but during this period he established himself as one of the greatest and most lovable Prime Ministers and leaders of India.

He belonged to a humble family, as his father Sharda Prasad was a poor man. He was born on October 2, 1904 at Mughal Sarai in Uttar Pradesh.

He joined the Harish Chandra High School at Varanasi where his uncle lived. Even at school, he was known for his intelligence, hard work, honesty and patriotic feelings, though physically he did not have much of an impressive personality, being short statured and thin.

He took an active part in the Non-Cooperation Movement and though he was arrested, he was not sent to jail, being teenaged and weak.

He got later education at Kashi Vidyapeeth. He was married to Lalita Devi when he was 24. He did great social work at the instance of Gandhi under whose influence he had come. He later went to imprisonment several times for offering *Satyagraha*. He studied a number of authors during his prison time.

He joined as Railway Minister in 1962 in Jawaharlal Nehru's cabinet. But taking moral responsibility for a railway accident, he resigned gracefully.

After Jawaharlal's death in 1964, he became the Prime Minister. He had to fight the war of 1965 with Pakistan. It was the time when his greatest sterling qualities of patriotism, courage and leadership came on the surface. He won the war and signed the Tashkent Agreement, but unfortunately he died of a massive heart attack on 11th January, 1966 while he was still at Tashkent. He will always be remembered as one of the greatest Indians.

LALA LAJPAT RAI

Lala Lajpat Rai was one of the greatest freedom fighters of India. He was popularly known as *Punjab Kesari*. He was a martyr who laid down his life for the freedom of India.

He was born at Dhudike in the Ferozepur district in Punjab on 28th January, 1865. His father Lala Radha Krishan was a school teacher. Lajpat Rai did his matriculation from Ambala in 1880 and joined the Government College, Lahore. He did law and started practice at Hissar. He became quite a successful lawyer.

Lajpat Rai had an inborn tendency to do social service and help others. He joined the Arya Samaj and started the work of social reforms. He was very much interested in educational matters. He founded a Sanskrit School at Hissar and took great pains to collect funds for starting the Dayanand Anglo Vedic (DAV) College at Lahore. He also did a lot of social work to help the famine victims in 1899.

He joined the Indian National Congress in 1888. In 1905, he and Gopal Krishna Gokhale were sent to England by the Congress to express the views of the party and the Indian people to the British rulers.

He was not only a great orator but a good writer also. He started "Young India", a monthly paper and wrote several books to arouse the Indian people to the necessity for demanding freedom from the British rule. He was also a great unionist and became the first President of the Indian Trade Union Congress. He was even jailed for his unionist views.

He later joined the Swarajist party which was started by Moti Lal Nehru and Deshbandhu C.R. Das. He was even elected to the Central Legislative Assembly on the ticket of this party.

The Simon Commission arrived in Lahore on 31st October, 1928. Like all the patriotic people, Lalaji objected to the Commission being all whites. He led a forceful but non-violent demonstration against the Commission. He was assaulted by Mr. Scott, a cruel British police officer and was given severe *lathi* blows. He died on 17th November, 1928 as a result of these *lathi* blows.

His last words are unforgettable. "Every blow hurled on me would prove a nail in the coffin of the British imperialism."

❏ ❏ ❏

F
HISTORICAL PERSONALITIES

ASHOKA–THE GREAT

Indian history reveals the heroic deeds of great men. One bright star of Indian history was the first emperor to follow the principles of Ahimsa, Love and Peace. My hero is none other than the Emperor Ashoka— The Great.

The grandson of Chandragupta and the son of Bindusar, Ashoka was brought up in Patliputra. In 273 BC he ascended the throne of the Mauryan Empire, founded by Chandragupta, with a desire to expand his kingdom and unite India under his only rule. He began his conquests winning each war like a brave soldier. The Kalinga war in 261 BC changed him completely. Seeing the great loss of lives and wealth he pledged never to wage war in future. The main factor that changed his heart was the self-immolation of a dancing woman from Kalinga who died fighting for him.

He devoted the rest of his life to the promotion of peace. He inspired people to be truthful, loving and dutiful. Though he adopted Buddhism and made it the state religion, he believed in religious tolerance. He also sent the priests to the neighbouring kingdoms for the spread of Buddhism. The numerous inscriptions found on the rocks and pillars tell us about his religious edicts.

He worked for the welfare of his subjects. He made new laws, appointed ministers and made justice common for all the sections of the society. All the social services were provided to the people. The improvement of roads and construction of shelter homes for the travellers led to the development of trade. In order to prevent cruelty to animals he banned animal slaughter throughout his kingdom. He devoted his life to the service to humanity and their well-being.

Art and sculpture also flourished under his rule. Even today, the Stupas at Gaya, Sarnath and Sanchi reflect his fine taste of architecture.

The Ashok Chakra and the Lions of the iron pillar hold their importance in our national flag and stamps. These two symbols always remind us of Ashoka's greatness.

Ashoka was a man of high learning. He had a strong character. He maintained friendly relations with the neighbouring kingdoms. He was the most respected Emperor who won the hearts of all his subjects. He really was "The Great".

CHHTRAPATI SHIVAJI

Shivaji was one of the greatest patriots of India whom the countrymen will not forget as long as the sun is there in the sky.

He was born on February 19, 1630. The name of his father was Shahaji Bhosle and the name of his mother was Jijabai. He was greatly influenced by his mother who was a highly religious lady. Dada Konda Dev was his guru.

Shivaji was a lover of martial arts and riding, wrestling, etc. even in his early boyhood. He also loved reading and writing. He was very fond of religious discourses and he daily listened to the sweet, enlightening religious hymns.

He was a great patriot who rejected the cruel Mughal rulers. The fanatic Aurangzeb was then the emperor.

Shivaji was just the ring leader of some diehard young men, but his influence on them was such that he turned his followers into a veritable army and started the process of capturing forts. Fort after fort fell before him and his brave young boys.

Just when he was 29, he had captured 40 forts and his army had swelled into a formidable force.

In order to teach a lesson to Shivaji, the ruler of Bijapur sent a huge army of 10,000 soldiers under Afzal Khan. But the latter was killed by Shivaji and many of his men were captured by him.

Later, Aurangzeb sent Shaista Khan. But he too was overpowered by Shivaji. However, at last Shivaji was captured by Aurangzeb's men. He was brought to Agra and imprisoned there. But Shivaji and his son, Sahu, escaped in the baskets of sweets which were taken out from the prison by the servants.

Shivaji conquered many areas and his kingdom comprised a big territory. He was crowned Chhatrapati in 1674. He breathed his last in 1680.

Shivaji's main plank, at least at the initial stages, was a guerrilla war. He was as shrewd and tactful as his enemy. But unlike the latter, he was not cruel.

He never tortured the captured soldiers. In particular, he was highly respectful to women. He did not harm them in any way but also protected their honour at all costs. He also gave full attention to the navy besides infantry. He worshipped the goddess Bhawani.

AKBAR–THE GREAT

Akbar was considered as the greatest Mughal Emperor. It was he who wanted both the Hindus and the Muslims to be united. He was a very generous and just ruler. Among the Mughal Emperors, he was the true ideal.

Akbar was born on October 15, 1542, at the Rajput Fortress of Umarkot in Sind, where the Mughal Emperor Humayun and his wife, Hamida Banu Begum were taking refuge. In 1540, Humayun had been driven into exile, following decisive battles, by the Afghan leader, Sher Shah. Akbar did not go to Persia with his parents, and was raised for a time instead by his uncle, Askari and his wife in the rugged country of Afghanistan rather than in the splendour of the Persian court. He spent his youth learning to hunt, run and fight, but he never learnt to read or write, the sole exception in Babur's line. Nonetheless, Akbar matured into a well-informed ruler, with refined tastes in the arts, architecture and music, a love for literature, and a breadth of vision that tolerated other opinions.

He succeeded his father, Humayun in 1556, and assumed power in 1560. The early years of his reign were marred by civil war and rebellion, but after triumphing over his enemies within the empire, he turned to foreign conquest, extending his control over the whole of North India. He reformed the tax system, promoted commerce, encouraged science, literature, and the arts, and abolished slavery. Although brought up as a Muslim, he pursued a tolerant and eclectic religious policy.

A magnetic personality and an outstanding general, he gradually enlarged his empire to include Afghanistan, Baluchistan, and nearly the entire Indian peninsula, north of the Godavari River. To unify the vast state, he established a uniform system of administration throughout his empire and adopted a policy of conciliating the conquered chieftains. Having defeated the Rajputs, the most militant of the Hindu rulers, he allied himself with them, giving their chiefs high positions in his army and government. Akbar also married Rajput princesses.

Akbar was a great patron of architecture, art, and literature. His court was rich in culture as well as wealth. In fact, his court was so splendid that the British monarch, Queen Elizabeth I, once even sent out her ambassador, Sir Thomas Roe, to meet the king! Many of Akbar's buildings still survive, including the Red Fort at Agra, and the city of Fatehpur Sikri, near Agra, which has a 10-km long wall encircling it.

Although he was himself illiterate, Akbar's courts at Delhi, Agra, and Fatehpur Sikri were centres of the arts, letters and learning. He was much impressed with the Persian culture.

Akbar founded his own religion, the *Din-i-Elahi* or the "Divine Faith". *Din-i-Elahi* as propounded by Akbar which combined mysticism, philosophy and nature worship. It did not recognise gods or prophets. The elitist religious cult had few followers. The only person other than Akbar who was a believer of *Din-i-Elahi* until death was Birbal, one of Akbar's ministers.

The last few years of Akbar's reign were troubled by the misconduct of his sons. Two of them died in their youth. The third, Salim, later known as Emperor Jahangir, was frequently in rebellion against his father. Asirgarh, a fort in the Deccan, proved to be the last conquest of Akbar, taken in 1599 as he proceeded north to face his son's rebellion.

Akbar keenly felt these calamities, and they may even have affected his health and hastened his death, which occurred in Agra in 1605. His body was interned in a magnificent mausoleum at Sikandra, near Agra.

MAHARANA PRATAP

Maharana Pratap was a great warrior and patriot in the regime of Mughal emperor Akbar.

✩✩ *Latest Essays & Letters* ✩✩

He took a vow to get back Chittor. A great battle was fought at Haldighati. The great Mughal army under the command of Man Singh and Prince Salim fought with Rana Pratap and his brave soldiers. Rana and his soldiers fought bravely to the last man. But at last they lost the field.

Maharana Pratap was born in the family of Shishodia Rajputs. His father Udai Singh was a man of character. Other Rajputs had given their daughters to Akbar. But Udai Singh did not do so. To avoid fight with Akbar he left Chittor.

Rana Pratap took a vow to make Chittor free from Mughals. He had now to run from-the place with his queen and children. He passed his bad days in the forests away from sharp eyes of Akbar. They ate wild fruits and sometimes had no food for a number of days. It throws light on his sufferings. Once the little princess was crying for food. The queen had nothing to prepare any food. In helplessness she prepared some loaves of grass and wild fruits. They ate the loaves and put one of them under a piece of stone for the princess who was sleeping. When she woke and began to eat loaf, a wild cat took the loaf away from her hand. There was no other loaf. The princess began to cry.

Now Rana Pratap decided to write a letter to Akbar. He wanted to surrender before him. But just then his old and faithful minister, Bhama Shah came to him and placed all wealth at his feet. He asked Rana to prepare a new Army to fight with Akbar.

❑ ❑ ❑

G

MUSICAL MAESTRO

USTAD BISMILLAH KHAN

Ustad Bismillah Khan was born on 21 March 1916 in village Dumraon of Bihar to a family of musicians who played for the local raja. Khan was sent to learn music from his uncle, Ali Bux 'Vilayati' who played the Shehnai at the Vishwanath temple in Varanasi. Here he learnt Hindustani genres like hori, dadra, chaiti and thumri and rendered them with skill and feeling on his Shehnai. He further developed forms like Khayal and explored classical ragas through elaborate alaap. His first concert was in Kolkata in 1924. Thereafter Khan burst on the world fully when he performed with his Shehnai solo at the prestigious Calcutta Music conference of 1937, after which his legend grew unstoppably.

His most piognant moment was when he played the Shehnai at the request of Pandit Jawaharlal Nehru to mark India's first Independence Day. His happiest moments were those spent playing for Kashi Vishwanath and for Sri Hanuman at the Sankat Mochan temple in Varanasi. He was a devotee of Godess Saraswati and lord Balaji. His day used to start at dawn with hours of riyaz on the steps of the Balaji ghat on the Ganga. Khan was a modest man with almost no wants and preferred to live a spartan life. His room on the top floor of his house had only a few things like a cot, a chair, an earthern pot for water and his shehnai.

He has played in Afghanistan, Europe, Iran, Iraq, Canada, West Africa, USA, USSR, Japan, Hong Kong and almost every capital city across the world. His choice of music was Raga Kafi which was usually dismissed as light and sensual but had deep Indian resonance everywhere.

Ustad Bismillah Khan had been honoured with various awards for his outstanding performance like Bharat Ratna, Padma Vibhushan, the Sangeet Natak Academi Award and the Tansen Award by Madhya Pradesh government. His honorary doctorate from Banaras Hindu University and Shantiniketan bespeaks of his fame.

The Shehnai that had heralded in independent India's first dawn was silenced on 21st August 2006. His last wish to perform at the India Gate in memory of martyrs remained unfulfilled. He died at Varanasi at the age of 90 years of cardiac arrest. He was burried at Fatman locality with full state honours.

The Ustad's music, however, endures to inspire national identity. Ustad Khan was credited with having almost monopoly over the instrument as he and shehnai are almost synonyms. His recital had almost become a cultural part of Independence Day celebrations every year. Despite his fame, his lifestyle retained its old world, Benares charm. A man of tenderness, he believed in remaining private and said that musicians are supposed to be heard and not seen. Ustad Khan will be remembered as one of the finest musicians in post-independent classical music and one of the best examples of Hindu-Muslim unity in India.

PANDIT RAVI SHANKAR

Pandit Ravi Shankar is a household name, for who does not know the great sitarist who has dominated the Indian music scene with his magical mastery of the sitar. One has only to witness him playing to recognise his genius, the quick, ease with which he handles this intricate instrument making him a master in the art of playing the strings. Ravi Shankar, has been one of the pioneers in popularising Indian music in foreign countries. Every performance of his in the USA, Europe and Australia, have been tremendously successful. He has composed music for foreign films and composed and conducted the music set to Pandit Nehru's 'Discovery of India'. During 1969-74, he composed the music for the Festival of India along with well known musicians from Europe and America. He also acted as Director of Music, All India Radio from 1949-55. Ravi Shankar was honoured by requesting him to compose the music for the IXth Asiad held in Delhi in 1982.

Born on 7th April, 1922 his initial training was under Ustad Alauddin Khan of Mahiar (1938-44). Because of his inborn talent and love of the sitar, Ravi Shankar received several prestigious awards and honours, both national and international. Some of them are : the international Music Vensco Award, Silver Bear, and Venice Festival Award. In 1976, he won the Presidential Award. Ravi Shankar was nominated to the Rajya

Sabha in 1986. In 1967, he opened the Klunara School of Music in Los Angeles (USA). Pandit Ravi Shankar died on December 11, 2012 in San Diego, California but he will remain alive forever in the heart of music lovers.

LATA MANGESHKAR

Who can ever forget her melodious voice that rule Indian cinema, whether it be a song of woe, or love, or spring–whenever, whatever, Lata Mangeshkar sang them all. She is also popularly referred to as the 'Nightingale of India' and continues to sing to data in Indian Cinema.

She has a place in the reputed Guinness Book of World Records as the singer with the highest number of songs to her credit. She has already sung over 30,000 songs in almost every Indian language.

Dinanath Mangeshkar, her father owned a theatrical company and was a reputed classical singer. However, when her father died in 1942, the onus of being the breadwinner of the family fell on Lata. Between 1942 and 1948, she acted in as many as eight films in Hindi and Marathi to take care of the family's economic problems. By 1950, the Lata wave had changed the industry. Her high-pitched singing rendered obsolete the heavy nasal voices of the day.

She is the recipient of several awards both in our country and abroad.

She was born on 28th September 1929, in Indore, Madhya Pradesh and learnt music as a child from her father. She has remained single and is extremely religious in her personal life. She holds a place that few can ever reach and remains the 'best', the music world has ever had.

A Dada Saheb Phalke Award winner for her contribution to Indian Cinema, the jewel in her crown in having India's highest civilian award, the Bharat Ratna (2001) conferred on her.

A.R. RAHMAN

A. R. Rahman, is an acclaimed composer, best known for composing film scores. This genius with his exceptional talent has reached heights of success that people of his age can only dream of.

Rehman made his debut in 1992 with Mani Ratnam's Tamil movie, *Roja* (Rose), which was subsequently dubbed into many languages including Hindi. He is a recipient of the Padma Bhushan, which is one of India's highest civilian national honours.

The musical maestro of Indian Cinema was born on January 6, 1966 in Madras, to a musically affluent family. He was born as A. S. Dileep Kumar to parents K. A. Sekhar, a music composer and mother Kasturi. He came to be known as A. R. Rahman later when the family converted to Islam. Rahman started learning piano at the tender age of four. He lost his father in his childhood. As a result, the pressure of supporting the family fell on young Rahman.

At the age of 11, he joined Illaiyaraja's troupe as a keyboardist. He also played on the orchestra of M. S. Vishwanathan and Ramesh Naidu and accompanied Zakir Hussain and Kunnakudi Vaidyanathan on world tours. The experience allowed him to obtain a scholarship at Trinity College of Music at Oxford University, where he received a degree in Western Classical Music.

In 1987, he got a chance to compose a jingle to promote Allwyn's new trendy range of watches. His work was appreciated and he got many more offers. He has done jingles for popular ads like Parry's, Leo Coffee, Boost, Titan, Premier Pressure Cooker, Asian Paints, etc. Rahman went on to compose more than 300 jingles and received awards and recognition for his work and he continued in advertising for five years.

In 1991, director Mani Ratnam, approached him and offered job as composer of music for his upcoming film *Roja*, at a price of Rs. 25,000. Rahman got the national award for the best music director that year. From then, there was no looking back for him. He got offers from a lot of directors of south and the Hindi film industry.

Apart from films, Rahman has also done compositions for patriotic albums like 'Vande Mataram' a tribute to the motherland released simultaneously in 28 countries across the world. He has received numerous awards in recognition of his talent. Rahman is conquering frontiers like few Indians have ever done. If the two Oscars he won in 2009 for 'Slumdog Millionaire' brought him worldwide fame, the two Grammy Awards he won on January 31, 2010 further cemented his place in the hearts of millions of music lovers across the globe.

On 4 October 2015, the government of Seychelles named A.R. Rahman *Cultural Ambassador for Seychelles* in appreciation of the "invaluable services contributed to enhance Seychelles' Arts and Culture development."

❏ ❏❏

H
THE GREAT SCIENTISTS

DR. APJ ABDUL KALAM

Dr. APJ Abdul Kalam served the nation as the 11th President of India during July 2002 to July 2007. A notable scientist and an engineer, he is often referred to as the 'Missile Man of India'.

Born on October 15, 1931 at Rameshwaram in Tamil Nadu, Dr. Avul Pakir Jainulabdeen Abdul Kalam, specialized in Aeronautical Engineering from Madras Institute of Technology. He was responsible for the evolution of the Indian Space Research Organisation's (ISRO) launch vehicle programme, particularly, the Polar Satellite Launch Vehicle (PSLV) configuration.

He had been awarded the coveted civilian awards—Padma Bhushan (1981) and Padma Vibhushan (1990) and the highest civilian award, Bharat Ratna (1997). He was a recipient of several other awards and fellow of many professional institutions. His 79th birthday was recognised as World Students' Day by United Nations.

On April 29, 2009, he became the first Asian to be bestowed with the Hoover Medal, America's top engineering prize, for his outstanding contribution to public service. He wrote four books— "India 2020–A Vision for the New Millennium" (1998), "Wings of Fire" (1999), "Ignited Minds–Unleashing the Power within India" (2002) and "My Journey: Transforming Dreams into Actions" (2013).

Dr. Kalam died in Shillong on July 27, 2015 while delivering a lecture. We, the people of India, will never forget his contribution in the making of modern India.

Dr. H.J. Bhabha

Homi Jahangir Bhabha was a pioneer of nuclear physics in his time and is considered the father of nuclear sciences in India. With the help of J. R. D. Tata, he established the Tata Institute of Fundamental Research at Mumbai.

Bhabha was born on October 30, 1909, into a wealthy Parsi family. He had a good library of science books at home and even as a child was interested in science. He used to spend his spare time in painting and writing poetry. He was also fond of music, particularly the Western classics. His father's ambition was to train Bhabha as an engineer and he was sent abroad for higher studies. However, his interest shifted to physics. During his studies abroad, he won many medals and fellowships. He also got the opportunity to work with eminent physicists like Enrico Fermi and Wolfgang Pauli.

He came into highlights in 1937, after his work in the area of cosmic rays. He later joined the Indian Institute of Science, Bangalore, and began to do research on cosmic rays, with huge retrievable plastic balloons carrying instruments high up in the sky. Cosmic rays revealed some revolutionary facts about the nature of matter and research.

Meanwhile, Bhabha was elected fellow of the Royal Society for his contributions relating to cosmic rays, elementary particles and quantum mechanics.

In 1945, the Tata Institute of Fundamental Research was set up. Two years later, when the country gained independence, his ideas gained more significance. Jawaharlal Nehru, the first Prime Minister, also wanted to make the country self-sufficient in science and technology and he gave Bhabha a free hand to do what he wanted.

In 1948, the Atomic Energy Commission was set up and Bhabha was made its Chairman. From then on, nuclear energy research has steadily gathered momentum in the country. Under the expert guidance of Bhabha, three atomic reactors, Apsara, Cirus and Zerlina, were built. Survey for uranium ore continued and plants to purify the required materials were also built. Construction of the country's first atomic power station began at *Tarapur* in 1963. Two years later, a plutonium plant was installed, which was hailed as a "great step". In short, Bhabha showed his countrymen and the world that Indians were second to none in gaining scientific knowhow. The climax came on May 18, 1974, when Indian scientists exploded a nuclear device for peaceful purpose at Pokhran in Rajasthan. India became the sixth country to join the nuclear club.

Bhabha also encouraged research in electronics, space science, radio astronomy and microbiology. The telescope at Ootacamund is one of his creations.

He was killed in an air-crash near the famous Mont Blanc peak of the Alps on January 24, 1966, while he was on his way to Vienna to attend a meeting of the Scientific Advisory Committee of the International Atomic Energy Agency. In 1967, the Atomic Energy Establishment, Trombay, was renamed the Bhabha Atomic Research Centre as a tribute to his dedication and work.

DR. C.V. RAMAN

C.V. Raman is one of the most renowned scientists produced by India. His full name was Chandrasekhara Venkata Raman. For his pioneering work on scattering of light, C.V. Raman won the Nobel Prize for Physics in 1930.

Chandrasekhara Venkata Raman was born at Trichinopoly in Southern India on November 7, 1888. His father was a lecturer in mathematics and physics so that from the very beginning, he was immersed in an academic atmosphere. C.V. Raman entered the Presidency College, Madras (now Chennai), in 1902, and in 1904 passed his BA examination, winning the first place and the gold medal in Physics. In 1907, he gained his MA degree, obtaining the highest distinctions.

His earliest researches in optics and acoustics - the two fields of investigation to which he has dedicated his entire career - were carried out while he was a student.

In 1917, he was offered the newly endowed Palit Chair of Physics at Kolkata University, and decided to accept it. After 15 years at Calcutta, he became Professor at the Indian Institute of Science at Bangalore (1933–1948). Raman also founded the *Indian Journal of Physics* in 1926, of which he was the Editor.

In 1922, Raman published his work on the "Molecular Diffraction of Light", the first of a series of investigations with his collaborators which ultimately led to his discovery of the radiation effect on February 28, 1928 and gained him the 1930 Nobel Prize in Physics.

Other investigations carried out by Raman were his experimental and theoretical studies on the diffraction of light by acoustic waves of ultrasonic and hypersonic frequencies (published in 1934-1942), and those on the effects produced by X-rays on infrared vibrations in crystals exposed to ordinary light.

Raman has been honoured with a large number of honorary doctorates and memberships of scientific societies. He was elected a Fellow of the Royal Society early in his career (1924), and was knighted in 1929. C.V. Raman died on November 21, 1970, at the age of eighty two.

VIKRAM SARABHAI

Vikram Sarabhai was one of the greatest scientists of India. He is considered as the 'Father of the Indian space program'. Apart from being a scientist, he was a rare combination of an innovator, industrialist and visionary.

Sarabhai was born on August 12, 1919 in Ahmedabad, India to an affluent, business family. He was one of eight children of Sarla Devi and Ambalal Sarabhai. After his studies at the Gujarat College at Ahmedabad, he left for England and joined St. John's College, Cambridge University where he received his undergraduate degree in 1940. In 1943, Vikram went up the Himalayan mountains to conduct experiments on cosmic rays under the tutelage of Nobel laureate Sir C.V. Raman. He was successful in his efforts, and was awarded a PhD by the Cambridge University in 1947 for his studies on this subject.

He studied cosmic rays under the Nobel laureate, Dr. C. V. Raman at the Indian Institute of Science (IISc), Bangalore from 1941 to 1945. He was instrumental in establishing the Physical Research Laboratory (PRL) in Ahmedabad in 1947.

After Dr. Homi Bhabha's demise, Dr. Sarabhai continued his work. Dr. A. P. J. Abdul Kalam, President of India (2002-2007), described it as his good fortune to work with Dr. Sarabhai.

The establishment of the Indian Space Research Organisation (ISRO) was one of his greatest achievements. He successfully convinced the government of the importance of a space programme for a developing country like India after the Russian, *Sputnik* launch. As a result of Dr. Sarabhai's dialogue with NASA, India launched the Satellite Instructional Television Experiment (SITE) during July 1975–1976.

Dr. Sarabhai was very interested in science education and founded a Community Science Centre at Ahmedabad in 1966. Today, the centre is called the Vikram Sarabhai Community Science Centre.

Dr. Bhabha supported Dr. Sarabhai in setting up the first rocket launching station in India. This centre was established at Thumba near Thiruvananthapuram on the coast of Arabian Sea, primarily because of its proximity to the equator. After a monstrous effort in infrastructure, personnel, communication links, and launch pads, on November 21, 1963, the inaugural flight was launched with sodium vapour payload.

Sarabhai commenced a project of fabrication and launching of an Indian satellite. As a result of this, the satellite, *Aryabhata* was put into orbit in 1975.

Dr. Vikram Sarabhai established many institutes which are of international repute. Most notable among them are IIMs(Indian Institute of Management) which are considered world class for their management studies.

He along with other Ahmedabad-based industrialists played a major role in the creation of the Indian Institute of Management, Ahmedabad.

He was married to the notable classical dancer, Mrinalini (Swaminathan) Sarabhai. They had a son, Karthikeya and a daughter, Mallika who went on to become a famous danseuse.

Vikram Sarabhai passed away in his sleep at a young age of 52 on December 31, 1971.

Dr. M.S. Swaminathan

DR. M. S. Swaminathan is India's most renowned agricultural scientist, who is closely associated with the Green Revolution in India. In recognition of his work, he has been awarded with the UNESCO Gandhi

Gold Medal in 1999, the Magsaysay Award, and the World Food Prize in 1987. He has been included by the Time magazine as one of the persons who has influenced the 20th century. He is the recipient of many national and international awards, including the Padma Vibhushan and the Albert Einstein World Science Award. Dr Swaminathan was also elected a Fellow of the Royal Society.

Born on August 7, 1925, Swaminathan graduated from Cambridge in 1952 with a Ph.D. in genetics. Swaminathan's contributions to the agricultural renaissance of India have led to his being widely referred to as the scientific leader of the green revolution movement.

He is married to Mina Swaminathan and has three daughters—Doctor Soumya Swaminathan, Kolkata based economist, Madhura Swaminathan and Nitya Rao, who works on Gender issues.

When he first joined the Indian Agriculture Research Institute, food production in India was not sufficient to meet its requirements and this was a major challenge for him. He formulated various schemes and projects to provide the benefit of research to the farmer in the field. He also introduced modern methods and techniques to raise agricultural production.

Swaminathan was the chairman of the UN Science Advisory Committee set up in 1980 to take the follow-up action on the Vienna Plan of Action. He has also served as an independent chairman of the FAO Council and president of the International Union for the Conservation of Nature and Natural Resources.

Dr. M.S. Swaminathan is a Fellow of the Royal Society of London and the US National Academy of Sciences. He currently holds the UNESCO Chair in Ecotechnology at the M. S. Swaminathan Research Foundation in Chennai (Madras), India. He is the chairman of the National Commission on Agriculture, Food and Nutrition Security of India.

He has been described by the United Nations Environment Programme as "the Father of Economic Ecology" and by Javier Perez de Cuellar, former Secretary General of the United Nations, as "a living legend who will go into the annals of history as a world scientist of rare distinction".

❏ ❏ ❏

I
SOCIAL ASPECTS/ISSUES

PATRIOTISM

We should remember that patriotism is essential to man, at least as long as the nation states are in existence.

The famous English poet belonging to Scotland, Sir Walter Scott wonders if there can be a man who does not love his motherland. He asks :

"Breathes there the man with soul so dead,

Who never to himself has said,

'This is my own, my native land."

A poet has rightly and most fervently said,

"I bow to thee my country,

All earthly things above."

It is something very simple. When even a pup or a kitten, being for a short while in a house, is taken to some distance and left at a lonely place, it tries its best to return to its original place. Then why should man be inferior even to a pup or kitten?

Man must prove himself to be superior to and higher than animals and birds. Thus a truly patriotic man, even when he lives in a foreign country, does not forget his native land.

We, indeed, should not forget our freedom fighters who made innumerable sacrifices for our freedom.

Earlier, in the First War of Independence, there emerged such leaders as Nana Phadnavis, Rani Lakshmi Bai of Jhansi, Bahadur Shah Zafar and others. Later, there appeared a galaxy of other patriotic leaders like Tilak, Gokhale, Tagore, Gandhi, Nehru, Pant, Maulana Azad and many others. Many of them had to spend the prime of their lives in British jails.

There were many martyrs like Sardar Bhagat Singh, Sukhdev and Rajguru who kissed death smilingly to attain freedom for us. Let us not forget them. Men like Subhash Chandra Bose and Chandra Shekhar Azad also made great sacrifices. Indeed, the list of true patriots and freedom fighters is too long to be capable of being given in detail here.

Unfortunately, after attainment of freedom, many of our leaders forgot the real purpose and they have been found involved in financial embezzlement and scandals and scams like the Bofors scam, fodder scam, telecom scam, the Hawala scam, etc. Many of them foment communalism or indulge in scams and scandals to amass huge wealth.

Let us all swear to be honest to our country that is just like our mother. That is why the word "Motherland" is used for one's native land. We call our country 'Mother India.' Let us be true to our mother and be ready to make any sacrifice for her and even be ready to lay down our lives for her sake. We should love all countries, indeed, the whole of mankind, while keeping the interests our own motherland uppermost in our mind.

Last but not the least, we should never forget the sacrifices of our freedom fighters made for the sake of the country. We must have generous hearts for the progeny of the martyrs. But it is most regrettable that in reality this does not happen.

Admiral Nelson, the famous English hero of the Battle of Trafalgar, had the following words painted on his battle-ship: "England expects every man to do his duty."

So, the crux of the point, regarding patriotism is to do one's duty. If we do well our duty assigned to us by our country, we are genuinely patriotic, otherwise our patriotism is fake and only skin-deep.

AN IDEAL CITIZEN

The word "Idealism" has attained some disdainful connotations in the modern world. It is because of the nefarious designs and most heinous activities of those whom the people at large hold in high esteem and who have proved unworthy of the task assigned to them.

Even then, it should not be construed that all the people have lost their good qualities and virtues. The common man, whatever he may be, is still kind, patriotic, compassionate and self-sacrificing at heart.

Still, it needs, not only good nature but some conscious efforts to be an ideal citizen. Thus, the first and foremost quality of an ideal citizen is that he is honest to the backbone, whatever his profession may be. He never cheats or lets others down. If he is a shopkeeper, he does not indulge in black-marketing nor does he give short measure of goods sold by him.

An ideal employee truly gives the worth of the salary he gets from the employer. He works sincerely and honestly all the time during his duty hours.

An ideal citizen is a highly disciplined person. He obeys his superiors giving full and genuine respect to them. Similarly, he never tries to bully those inferior to him. He may give them orders in a commanding manner, no doubt, but he never talks to them in a rude manner. He is full of politeness and consideration. He has a very high regard for others' feelings and sentiments. Just as he is frank in giving his candid opinion, advice and suggestions to his superiors, he is likewise ready to accept others' sound advice or suggestions with an open heart and for the benefit of all concerned.

An ideal citizen is a model of punctuality and regularity. If he is a student, he goes to his school or college punctually and attends every period. He does his homework regularly. He obeys his parents and teachers and has genuine respect and regard for them.

An ideal citizen has full consideration for the comfort and convenience of senior citizen. He does everything within his means to help the aged, the children, the women, the handicapped and those in a helpness or disadvantageous position.

An ideal citizen has the physical courage to face the bullies or those who harass the weak, the helpless and the infirm. He has the moral courage to own responsibility and accept his own shortcomings and point out others errors to them frankly.

An ideal citizen has a great civic sense. He does not spread pollution of any kind. He does not waste water, food, money or electricity.

He takes a balanced diet and also takes care of his health in every possible way, just as taking regular walks, exercise, etc.

He has no bad habits such as drinking, smoking, gambling, drug-consumption etc. But he takes interest in healthy sports, games both indoor and outdoor and may view healthy movies and serials.

He is a very dynamic person and he tries to do social service and help others whenever and wherever he can and in whatever reasonable and legal way he can. He is ready to do small sacrifices for others such as paying small amounts to the needy, paying bus fares to those who forget their purses at home, etc.

He helps the country at the time of a crisis or disaster, as he is imbued with the spirit of patriotism. He goes to the flooded areas or areas affected by an earthquake or storm and helps the people not only with money and material but also by doing social service. He may also have the daily routine of going to some hospital, lepers' colony or orphanage to help the needy in any way he possibly can. He takes the accident victims to the hospital.

He helps even the animals and birds if he finds them wounded or in distress.

He helps in the national policies of controlling population, health programmes such as pulse polio, AIDS control, TB and malaria management, literacy, drug-trafficking control, blood donation and eye camps, raising funds for poor children, riot and war victims, etc.

He takes interest in schemes regarding pollution control, removal of poverty, eradication of dowry system, law and order problems, begger problem, school dropouts problem, etc.

Last but not least, he pays all his taxes regularly and persuades others also to do so. He helps in managing scams, scandals, etc.

He may become a member of one or more societies that work in national, human and social interest with such aims as "bio-diversity mapping, effects of pollution on surface as well as ground water resources, conservation of existing wetlands, forests and wildlife, economic valuation of natural resources and disaster management and environment awareness among masses."

SOCIAL WELFARE

It is the foremost duty of every citizen to do some good to his country in one or the other field.

If somebody takes interest in doing good to the people by taking part in certain welfare programmes that sort of step taken by him should be appreciated. It is not that only an individual can do good deeds. Sometimes, the steps taken by a state government for the welfare of the poor people are highly appreciable.

Programmes and packages for social welfare should also be arranged by all states across the country. Of course, a silent social revolution is taking place in India, but we also have to admit that "Delhi is a far cry." But also we have to remind ourselves that "Rome was not built in a day."

Most of the developed countries have great social safety valves which keep the citizens entirely tension-free as far as simple livelihood or bread and butter is concerned. Unfortunately, in India such measures are lacking.

The Western countries, of course, being afraid of the rapidly spreading communism, had to resort to such social welfare measures as unemployment allowance, old age pension, brilliant student freeships, etc., and had to enhance substantially the provision from the national budget for raising the standard of education, improvement of people's health, child and maternity care, improvement of the lot of the poor, housing problem, more attention to prisons, institutions, clubs, health centres, youths' problems, etc. But whatever the occasion, the western countries have given great relief to the common man who can have a sound sleep with the assurance that he and his children won't have to go hungry, naked and houseless whatever the circumstance is in his life.

In India, we are virtually devoid of any social safety measures, though some schemes have been started. The Nehru Rojgar Yojna and the Prime Minister's Rojgar Yojna are really useful schemes.

There are schemes like old-age pension scheme and the supply of wheat and rice at cheap rates to those below the poverty line. Such schemes are indeed, commendable. But, it is a pity that even in such cases, the agents, bookies and touts gobble up the major amount and the money and goods meant for the poor and needy never reach the deserving ones. Large-scale scams regarding old-age pensions and others are being unearthed but the culprits are either not caught or hardly punished adequately, if at all. That is why we are witnessing scam after scam and there seems to be no end to scam and scandals. What a pity! This great country of ours "Our Bharat Mahan" has been turned into a land of scams and all that corruption carries in its train.

There are several schemes for the Dalits, the farmers and the students. In Punjab and certain other states, some help in the form of a "Shagun," etc. is given to the dalit parents at the time of the marriage of their daughter. On the birth of a child, some money is given to a poor mother for diet and other expenses. In the matter of housing and installing flush latrines in their homes, financial help is provided to the Dalits by the government. The farmers are given free electricity in Punjab. The students can get easy loans at low rates of interest for pursuing studies in India and abroad.

Similarly, there are other schemes. But the common man is not getting much benefit as yet. It is because of two main reasons. One, the help is inadequate. For example, a common man who knows no skill cannot get the benefit of starting a new venture by getting a loan, the major part of which has finally to be returned. Secondly, whatever help is even made available, is pocketed by a few influential people at the top by presenting bogus people as the needy ones.

Thus, we have still to go a long way in the matter of social welfare. We have to work hard bearing in mind the famous lines of the renowned American poet, Robert Frost:

"Woods are lovely, dark and deep,

But I have promises to keep,

And miles to go before I sleep,

And miles to go before I sleep."

CORRUPTION IN INDIA

Corruption is one of the most horrible problems across the world. It has spread its roots quite deep in the Indian society also. Corruption means bribery or illegal gratification. It is a great blow to the honest persons who love certain good principles. This horrible problem is eating away our values of life. J.L. Nehru had said, "A corrupt official should be hanged on the nearest lamp-post."

The main cause of corruption is that every person wants easy money to become rich overnight. Most of the bureaucrats and ministers in our country indulge in this process. They are never afraid of any law or any sort of penalty.

So many scams have taken place in India. But the criminals are still at large and are mocking at the laws of our country. In a short spell of time we have had the shares scam, the fodder scam, the sugar scam, the Bofors scam, the Hawala scam, the telecom scam, 2G scam and coalgate scam, etc.

Even CBI is unable to recover or trace the amount thus lost.

Almost all departments in India are corrupt. There are illegal fees in every department. If you want to get any of your problems solved even if it is a genuine problem, you have to grease the palms of officials.

Files in offices do not move without bribe. A stage appears to have come in which people take corruption for granted. In this regard one thing is sure and this is that our society has a great regard for those who are rich. We never bother the way through which the man has earned so much.

So, this measuring of a person by the amount of wealth he possesses, has made the world materialistic. Everybody is running after luxuries like car, air conditioner, a well-decorated house and so on, and to attain such items he applies every formula, which may lead to corruption, also called bribe.

When our leaders or ministers are corrupt and we consider them our guides, the society learns a lot from them and people get the motto to earn money by hook or by crook.

Many other factors are black marketing, poverty, lack of awareness among the people, unemployment, burgeoning population, price rise etc. All these factors together give birth to corruption.

If the government seriously wants to have a good society, strict laws have to be passed and the guilty have to be dealt with severely. Otherwise, no one can check a revolution which may ultimately come off in this country.

How strange it is that the industries become sick but not the industrialists. They flaunt their wealth even more openly. The result is that the money needed for public health, education, sanitation, employment opportunities, social security, etc., is gobbled up by these sharks.

It is thus quite clear that even in the matter of corruption the root cause is the lack of awakening among the masses. It is the respectability that the corrupt get in society that makes them ever more corrupt and others who may not otherwise like to be corrupt, follow in their footsteps. If the people look down upon the corrupt and even have a social boycott of them, the corrupt may cease to be so. Moreover, it takes two to make a quarrel. If the people refuse to pay the bribe, corruption will die its own natural death.

ENVIRONMENTAL POLLUTION

Air pollution is caused when the required quantity (volume) of oxygen in air gets depleted and the quantity (volume) of other gases like carbon dioxide, sulphur dioxide, nitrogen, etc. gets inordinately increased. This can happen because of several factors, some of which are noted below:

The balance of oxygen in atmosphere is maintained mainly by the trees. Ideally in India, we should have about 33% of our area covered by lush green forests. But we have only about 23 per cent of such area. In certain States, as in Punjab, such area may be much less.

We know that trees absorb carbon from the air in sunlight and release carbondioxide. The process is known as photosynthesis. If we cut down trees ruthlessly, actually we bring about our own doom closer. So, instead of cutting down trees, we should grow more of them. If a single tree has to be cut down for one reason or the other, we must plant at least two in its place. We should take an active part in the festival of afforestation which aims at growing more and more trees during the summer and rainy seasons.

Air is also polluted by the automobiles working on leaded fuel and smoke from chimneys of factories. All such things should be controlled for the purpose of keeping pollution within the permissible limits.

The Punjab and Haryana High Court, taking a serious view of the problem of pollution in the steel town of Mandi Gobindgarh in Punjab, directed the Punjab Pollution Board as under:

"Any unit found not adhering to the pollution norms would not be allowed to become operational. In case it is found that the pollution standards have been violated by any unit or establishment, the Board and its officials would act swiftly against the erring units".

A kind of awakening in the matter of pollution is already there. In Delhi, the Supreme Court has banned the use of buses and automobiles running on diesel and has ordered that they must be allowed to run only on Compressed Natural Gas (CNG) which does not cause pollution.

Ambient air analysers should be set up in all major towns to know the quality of particles of carbon dioxide, nitrogen and sulphur dioxide in the air.

Water pollution is mainly caused when the toxic effluents from factories as from paper and sugar mills find their way in the rivers flowing down to the seas. Sometimes, the spilling of oil and other toxic matter from the sinking ships on the seas can also cause water pollution and lead to death of sea life on a large scale.

Soil pollution is caused by several agents including the reckless use of pesticides and insecticides. Thus excess of toxic matter in the soil enters the crops and vegetables. The excessive spraying of insecticidal medicines also makes vegetables and fruits toxic and unfit for human consumption.

The main factors responsible for noise pollution are: inessential use of high-pitch mikes and loud speakers and firing of crackers, horns, hooters, buzzers, etc. Some people are in the habit of keeping their T.V. sets and transistors at a high pitch, thus disturbing the neighbours, particularly the students and patients suffering from different ailments.

The main cause of space pollution is the circulation of innumerable spaceships and rotating objects hurled in space by several countries. Such artificial, satellites get disintegrated after their destined life and their parts get scattered in space.

Nowadays, there is pollution even on the high mountains. On the Siachen Glacier there is a large quantity of garbage because of the stationing of our troops which is unavoidable. On the entire way to the highest peak in the world, Mount Everest, the passage is littered with garbage left by the climbers.

Sometimes, a new type of pollution is caused when a nuclear reactor starts leaking. This causes what may be termed nuclear pollution which causes radiation leading to ailments like cancer, retarded growth among children etc.

Such leakages whether in nuclear reactors or factories, or solvent boilers etc. should be taken seriously. It was, after all, the Union Carbide poisonous gas leakage which caused the infamous Bhopal Gas tragedy which led to the loss of thousands of lives. Safety measures of all such plants should be properly and constantly taken care of.

CLEAN INDIA DRIVE

Prime Minister Narendra Modi launched the Swachch Bharat sanitation programme on October 2, 2014. It was a befitting tribute to the Father of the Nation who was concerned about sanitation issues. The proposed sanitation programme will reframe the social and economic face of India and prove to be a great game changer. Sanitation has a direct link with the spread of communicable diseases which are prevalent in India. The basic cause of frequent epidemics in India is insanitation. The country can attain Health for All by October 2, 2019, if the programme is implemented in totality.

Living in an insanitary environment, like poverty, degrades the quality of human life and it is a curse and a social stigma as well. Therefore, the accomplishment of the total Sanitation Programme (TSP) will improve the living standard of the poorest of the poor on the one hand and improve the Human Development Index (HDI) of India on the other. Presently, India is positioned 131 in the UN's HDI. Poverty is less painful if one gets a chance to live in a sanitary environment. In fact, a sanitary environment is the basic necessity of human life like air, water and food for its aesthetic and psychological development. That is why we say, "Cleanliness is next to godliness". If India ensures total sanitation by 2019, our stock will rise in the comity of nations.

Up to the 1960s, carrying human excreta as head load was the worst social stigma. Now open defecation has taken its place. Women go for nature's call at night in the open and they are frequently molested and even raped. The coverage for use of in-house sanitary latrines varies from state to state, depending upon the percentage of BPL families.

According to the proposed Swachh Bharat scheme, the government will build individual toilets in 1.04 crore households and 5 lakh community/public toilets in urban areas. Around 8.8 crore toilets will be built in rural areas and a majority of these are to be provided in individual households. The total sanitation programme includes programmes that are to be executed under the umbrella programme.

Provision of 100 per cent sewerage and a drainage system in all urban towns together with innocuous disposal or recycling of the finally treated effluent for irrigation with a total ban on discharge into the drains or rivers. An effective sewerage and drainage system forms the backbone of urban sanitation.

There is need for 100 per cent solid waste management, both in urban and rural areas and recycling of the final waste product. Around 100 per cent coverage of rural households and slum areas with sanitary latrines. All the open areas in urban and rural communities will be either paved or grassed. All the streets to be paved with concrete blocks or paver blocks. There should be zero tolerance to dumping or littering of solid waste matter (mostly paper and plastic matter) in open spaces, both in urban and rural areas. It should be the same for stagnation of sullage or any other waste water in urban or rural areas. There should be daily sweeping of streets, roads or public places both in rural and urban areas. The vacant plots should be provided with boundary walls and kept neat, clean and green.

Pursuit of Swachh Bharat also requires strengthening public health services. Services such as good drainage systems, absence of swamps and ponds that are home to stagnant water, and the supply of safe drinking water—all of which reduce exposure to and spread of diseases—are classic examples of public goods and require effective government intervention. Swachh Bharat would do well to encourage each state to restart a separate public health department, accountable for the delivery of public health services.

POPULATION EXPLOSION

In population, India is the second largest country of the world. The population of our country is above 1.21 billion. The population of our country is increasing at an alarming rate. We add the entire population of Australia every year to our population. We have reached a stage of population explosion.

There are various factors behind this sorry state of affairs. Most important among them is illiteracy. The government has fixed the minimum marriageable age for a boy as 21 years and a girl as 18 years. But in states like Bihar, Orissa, Rajasthan, etc. people never bother about this. Hence, child marriages are still common. Child marriage is a great factor for the rapid growth of population in India.

The other factor is that the illiterate people think that by adding more members to their families they will get more earning hands.

Being too poor many people have not still got the approach to T.V., etc. for entertainment and instructive purposes. So, these poor people find recreation only in sexual indulgence. This also leads to increase in population.

Another factor is the reduction in the death rate. The progress in medical science has also reduced the death rate. It is supposed that in the coming days, death rate will be reduced further due to the eradication of epidemics like plague, malaria, cholera etc. As a result, the problems of food, clothing, shelter, medicines, education etc. will aggravate still further.

The other main factor, which is responsible for the increase in population is ignorance and superstitions of the people, in particular of those who live in villages and in poor states. They do not believe in applying the family planning methods and think that the children are the gifts from God.

To our great surprise, India is an important producer of milk, vegetables, fruit, wheat, and rice but we are unable to export on a largescale these items that they could earn a lot of foreign exchange for our country. It is because we are too many in number to spare these items.

Hence population is one of the most horrible problems in India. The Government has taken a number of steps in this direction to tackle this problem. The family planning devices are given free of cost in the government hospitals and dispensaries. The government is trying its best to give at least the primary education to all. So that every citizen can understand his responsibilities and rights towards the country.

There is no denying the fact that although millions of births have been averted in India through the family planning programme, yet the programme has gone awry and we have not been able to achieve the desired results. To achieve the desired result, the poor uneducated people should be awakened on large scale through spread of education and mass media.

The youth should be involved in this campaign. The idea of usefulness of a small family should be installed into minds of youngsters.

POPULATION AS RESOURCE

Problem of Population Explosion in India has proved to be a big hindrance in the success of economic planning and economic development. Poverty, unemployment, low standard of living in India is, to a large extent, the consequences of population explosion. The vast majority of the Indians are barely able to read and write. This would appear to most people to be a major disaster, a population so large that the economy will, sooner or later, collapse under the weight of these numbers. However, so far it has not. In fact, the country is actually producing more food than it needs, and is consequently able to export rice and wheat. That we still have people dying of starvation in Odisha and Rajasthan is not because there is not enough; it is a terrible instance of the failure of the administrative system in these States, where godowns are full and yet the bureaucracy is unable to provide enough to people to keep them alive.

Having said this, however, one needs to go back a little to the country's huge population and ask if it is necessarily something that ought to cause panic and hysteria. In the early 1980s, Julian Symons wrote in his book The Ultimate Resource that the per capita income was likely to be higher with a growing population than with a stationary one, both in developed and undeveloped countries. The argument was that, even though it cost more to educate more children, eventually there would be a larger number of educated and productive young people, and even if there are two or three truly ingenious and creative people among a hundred of them it would be better if the population was larger than smaller for obvious reasons.

The key is here. This is what needs to be understood. If the education given to our young is even tolerably worthwhile, the results will inevitably augur well for the country. We need not look with apprehension at the flight of bright young people to more prosperous countries; there will be a good number in the country to develop the economy in different ways. That brings us to another question - the use of natural resources. It is true that the current patterns of consumption involve a larger use of natural resources, but a good part of this is really the result of patterns of consumption in earlier decades.

One needs to repeat that the key is education. It is time that our rulers and policy-makers paid more attention to this, and less to running airlines, hotels and other services. Educate our young and we will have created over time the most valuable resource a country can have - a population of young, creative people, aware of what is possible and what is not, what is destructive and what is sustaining and nurturing. If we invest half as much here as we are now doing in fields which fetch us nothing, we will have secured the future of the country.

One is not for a moment saying that the efforts to control population growth should stop, far from it. More determined and imaginative efforts are needed to make people actually take steps to limit their families. But we must make the best of what we already have, the huge numbers which will not go away. Instead of wringing our hands we could take some steps to make living with these billions a workable proposition and not a disaster.

GLOBALISATION

The modern world looks like a small village, while our house looks like the whole world. We have the winds of globalisation sweeping every nook and corner of the world.

Now, we have, in this age of Information Technology (IT), satellites, bearing their invisible rays, transmitted from the earth itself, to the receiving stations, T.V. sets, computers and telephone and other such systems all over the world.

The world has become one market and goods are transported and tranferred from one part of the world to the other through quick means of transport.

All kinds of goods from the remotest corners of the world lie at our door. Such are computers, garments, toys, pens, switches, TVs refrigerators, washing machines, steel and cement. Indeed, the choice rests with us.

And all these goods are at reasonable prices. But, all the same, the developing countries like India, have also been confronted with several problems, many of which seem intractable unless some remedial measures are taken.

At present, India is facing many serious problems. One of them is the problem of unemployment. It is said that more than 4.4 crore people are unemployed and many more underemployed in India at present.

There may be many reasons for this malaise. Globalisation is one of them. Our former prime minister late Narsimharao had introduced globalisation to our economy with a view to increase job opportunities to our crores of unemployed and underemployed people. It was said that globalisation would bring more jobs. But that has not actually happened. With the advent of computers and so many other machines and devices, thousands of workers, both skilled and unskilled, have been thrown out of their jobs.

Mahatma Gandhi had long warned us of the impending danger of the craze for machines. He said, "What I object to is the craze for machinery, not machinery as such. The craze is for what they call labour saving machinery. Men go on saving labour till thousands are without work and thrown on the open streets to die of starvation."

It must be noted that those who professed the benefit of the common people, did not actually mean it. Now, when thousands have been thrown on the open streets, the powers that be, are not much bothered, except for a mere lip-service.

Gandhiji's words are still very relevent when he says, "I want to save time and labour, not for a fraction of mankind but for all. I want the concentration of wealth, not in the hands of a few but in the hands of all." What do we see today? Is wealth in the hands of all? No. It is in the hands of a few.

It does not mean that we were wrong in accepting globalisation. There is nothing wrong with globalisation. Whatever wrong it is only with ourselves. The defect and deficiency lie in our own character, in our own ethical sense. Had we been honest, we would have devised some remedial measures right in the beginning. We have not devised any safety valves. We have developed no alternative means to absorb the surplus labour and staff. Those people who are relieved of their jobs could prove an asset if they were provided alternative jobs.

Indeed, we can still do so, only if we have the will and mind to do so.

Closely connected to globalisation is the concept of privatisation which is at present being followed in India. The logic is that through privatisation, we can achieve much more efficiency. This is perhaps correct in its own way, But, in the name of downsizing, adaptation, adjustment, perfection, stream-lining, justification, etc. many people are declared surplus.

If proper steps are taken regarding the drawbacks in the systems like privatisation and globalisation, the concepts do not deserve to be rejected downright. They may, prove a boon if they are implemented in right earnest keeping in mind the welfare of all concerned and not just a few.

We should be particularly cautious now when we are passing through the second generation of reforms regarding globalisation. One important benefit which we have derived to some extent and can derive much more from globalisation is the transfer of technology concerning research in various fields, for instance, in the matter of genetic engineering and biotechnology. Let us take full advantage of globalisation in the right spirit.

UNEMPLOYMENT

At present, our Employment Exchanges have registers containing long lists of unemployed youth. There are skilled, unskilled and educated youth who are unemployed. As per Employment Exchanges, there are more than 4.4 crore people unemployed and many more underemployed in India at present.

The educated ones run after white collared jobs which are hard to seek because of fewer jobs, reservations, glut of the qualified people, corruption, nepotism, favouritism and so many other factors. Our universities are turning out graduates like nuts and bolts in factories.

There is a glut of not only arts graduates, but also commerce, engineering, medical and other graduates in several technical, technological and managerial fields and disciplines.

However, there are emerging on the horizon, thanks to globalisation and Information Technology revolution, several new diplomas and courses which can help the young people to become proficient in them and get alternative jobs. But all the people cannot avail themselves of this opportunity. It is because they lack awareness, will, means, resources, guidance, etc.

The problem of unemployment can be solved only if our government and the society are both seriously interested in doing so. The upper class, to which the bureaucrats, politicians and industrialists of our country belong, is getting a whopping chunk of the exchequer in the form of pay, profits and other facilities. The bureaucrats' pay scales may be cut down and with the amount saved the unemployed can feed their families.

At present, whereas unemployment in general is a serious problem, higher posts are manned by either rich and powerful families, or persons from reserved categories. Those who are economically weaker and do not fit in any reserved category have been left high and dry.

The problem of unemployment can be solved by bringing about a comprehensive planning system for many years may be, two decades or so, keeping in view the likely rise in population and expected changes in the social set-up and scientific and other spheres.

The best way is to start new courses which are relevant to the times. New development schemes both in urban and rural areas should be started. The youth should be employed there.

Some self-financing schemes should also be started. The youths should be given liberal loans on easy terms to start their own enterprises on small-scale. Such youths should be provided free training and guidance and supervision in starting and running their plants at suitable places.

It is in the fitness of things that the government have already started some useful *Rozgar Yojna.* But in India there is still much scope for development. In rural areas in certain states, conditions are pretty bad. In slum areas almost everywhere, they are far from satisfactory.

Young people should be sent to work in slum areas, health resorts, rural development works, illiteracy, poverty, disease eradication programmes. For this, they must be paid adequately. Some means should be adopted for their absorption or rehabilitation in one or the other field, as the case may be, keeping in view their qualifications, experience, aptitude, family circumstances, etc.

THE STATUS OF WOMEN IN SOCIETY

No doubt, women deserve a better deal from society as they are getting at present. It is to be borne in mind that women are in no way inferior to men. Even some of the hymns of the sacred Vedas are said to have been written by women.

In ancient India, women occupied a very respectable place in society. No ritual could be considered perfect without the participation of some women in it. It is said that once when Lord Rama had to perform a *yagna* in the absence of Sita who was imprisoned in Ravana's Ashok Vatika, he had to place her statue made of gold to serve the purpose.

In the good olden days, women enjoyed much freedom. They could choose their own husbands. The ceremony was called "*Swayamvar.*" Sita *Swayamvar* and Sanyogita *Swayamvar*" are still remembered for their great historical or mythological value. In those days, women were highly educated. They took part in dancing and singing. They wore beautiful clothes and ornaments and fresh flowers in their hair and had sufficient freedom of movement.

It was during the middle ages that women began to be considered inferior beings and were ordained to live behind the four walls of their houses. Then they had to do strenuous household chores with no wages except simple food and clothing. They had alone to take all the care regarding rearing of children. They were given no share in the parental property or in the property of their husbands or inlaws. Their life was full of misery. They were illiterate and had no access to a school. Not much attention was given to their health. In states like Rajasthan, women had even to die on the pyre of their husbands.

The women were expected to show complete fidelity to their husbands. Moreover, they could never think of divorce.

Such a situation still continues more or less in the poor families and in rural areas.

On the contrary, in foreign countries, women have got much freedom. In certain countries like Italy, this excessive freedom is being misused, as there have developed certain women mafias which kill women and children. In the movement 'Women's Lib' that came into existence in the seventies, men were made targets of women's wrath.

In India, now, a great attention is being given to the welfare and progress of women. They have got equal opportunities with men. There can be no discrimination against women in the matter of education or employment. They have got their voting rights. Some institutions and universities give special rights to women to appear in certain examination privately, certain state governments give financial help to women on their marriage or for their maintenance if they have none else to support them.

At present, a small section of women has got freedom and such women are outdoing men in almost every field. Most of the women, particularly in the rural areas are illiterate and have no idea of their rights. Very aptly does a writer say:

"May be the saddest thing about India is that there is so much talk and so little action. The very best example in the position of women. Dr. Radhakrishnan once wrote that in the art of suffering, we men, are mere amateurs; it is the women who are the professionals. Just take a look at the system in society. In a poor country the only visible asset of a family is land. And in land, the women get nothing. They do not get individual ownership and have no claim to the homestead."

FARMERS' SUICIDE

Agriculture in India is the predominant occupation of the majority. With more than half of the population depending on agriculture as primary occupation, India is the second largest country in terms of arable area. However, farmers in India, like many other countries, are bound to live an intensely hard life. In spite of being feeders of the entire nation, they live in misery and poverty, which many times leads them to end their lives.

Causes of Farmers' Suicide

The primary cause of farmers' suicide is their poverty. The inception of miserable condition of farmers dates back to the colonial era when the British imposed hard hitting revenue system. Be it Permanent Settlement, Ryotwari or Mahalwari, all were aimed at extracting more and more revenue. This exorbitant revenue created a new class of moneylenders. After independence, efforts have been made by government for farmers to end the vicious cycle of debt trap by controlling moneylenders, yet this system is quite prevalent in villages. A major reason for this is inability of government to provide financial benefits to needy farmers through institutional means. Instead it has been found that a major portion of institutional loans is taken by big and rich farmers who instead use it for non-agricultural purpose. In the absence of institutional loans, small farmers are forced to go to moneylenders, who usually charge more interest. However, in case of crop failure or low price for crops, when these farmers are unable to repay loan, they are harassed, which many times forces them to end their life. Another big reason for the poverty of farmers is their unawareness towards what crop to grow according to the weather and soil condition, which may pay them high. Below threshold production or crop failure brings low to no remunerations, which causes piling up of interest on the loans taken. This again brings heavy exploitation of the farmers, again forcing them to end their life.

NATIONAL INTEGRATION

India is a multi-racial and multi religious country. It is a plurist State. It is a secular country where the people of all religions worship, without any let or hindrance, according to their religious practices, though subject to law and order.

Geographically and linguistically, India has a vast variety. It is a unity in diversity. The Indian people in different States and regions eat different kinds of food. They wear different clothes. They speak different languages. They have different castes and they observe different religious practices. Still, they are all Indians.

It is a pity that communal riots take place in different parts of our country off and on. Mostly, the innocent, gullible people are incited by political leaders and religious bigots to indulge in acts of violence and resort to arson, murder, loot, mayhem, etc.

The result is untold loss to life and property, mostly of innocent people. Such people should be dealt with sternly.

An awakening and love for the country should be brought about among the common people. These are the innocent illiterate people who are most gullible and most likely to be led astray. Therefore, the literacy campaign should be intensified.

Intercaste and inter-religious marriages should be less encouraged. People should be encouraged to celebrate together festivals sacred to all religions. Ancient monuments whether temples or mosques should be considered national monuments.

Students should be given patriotic lectures in colleges and the school and college curricula should include lives of great national leaders. Practice of pilgrimages, fairs, etc. where members of all communities participate should be encouraged.

Dowry System

Dowry system is one of the oldest institutions in India. It was prevalent in the sprawling Vijayanagar Empire in South India in medieval times.

Although the dowry system took its birth in the hoary past, yet it has conspicuously become a nuisance in the modern age. It is mainly because the world has gone the whole hog towards materialism and the ever-increasing greed and avarice in the minds of the people has been the net result.

It is not unoften that we read and hear about dowry tortures and deaths. The girls are harassed by their Mammon-worshipping in-laws. They are asked to bring more and more dowry. In some cases even the constant flow of money and material objects from the bride's side cannot quench thirst of the money-loving bridegroom's kith and kin.

In earlier times, the items given to the bridegroom and his kith and kin as dowry were such as land, cattle, livestock, cash, jewellary, etc.

Still later, entered the realm of dowry such items as cars, scooters very costly furniture, refrigerators, T.V. sets, VCRs, etc.

In all cases, cash money, jewellery and clothes were important components of dowry. As far as cash is concerned, previously, it was limited to a few hundred rupees, then a few thousand rupees and now it is in lakhs of rupees and in more affluent societies, even in crores of rupees. Rarely, we hear of even big buildings, bungalows, gardens, farms, meadows and such things also transferred as items of dowry.

Isn't all this ridiculous and a total negation of all the cultural values we so proudly undertake and claim to have? More so, when the poor girl and her parents are forced to gorge out so much when they have already spent a lot on the girl's upbringing and education and on her marriage in the form of a sumptuous feast under an expensive stall or in a luxurious hotel or marriage palace and in distribution of sweets and various gifts to so many relatives on both sides?

Is it not the height of cruelty to force the poor girl and her parents to spend all this even when they are not in so comfortable a financial position and have to undertake heavy debts, and girl's educational, and other merits, are considered secondary only?

Sometimes, all this mad race for money on the parts of the bridegroom's parents and others leads to the suicide of the poor girl. Sometimes, a poor lonely creature is put to flames alive by her heartless, ruthless in-laws.

Of course, there are a number of Anti-Dowry laws but they are hardly ever implemented. The social organisations should force the government to bring to book all recalcitrants. Media should take up the task of bringing about an awakening among the youth of country. In schools and colleges, all boys should take an oath that they would not demand any dowry at the time of their marriage. Likewise, all girls should take an oath that they should not marry a dowry-seeking boy, come what may.

We should also bear in mind the obverse side of this coin. Taking advantage of the Anti-dowry laws, sometimes some clever girls try to harass their inlaws for no fault of theirs and in such cases often the girls' parents are also behind them, instigating them into doing such an unholy act.

CO-EDUCATION

In the system of co-education girls and boys study together under the same roof. There is however, a controversy whether co-education should be there or not. There are different views. Some speak in favour of it while others speak against this system of education.

Those who favour it, give their reasons openly. They consider both men and women equal in all walks of life. And they hold that men and women have to work in the same offices, in the same business houses, etc. Not only this, both men and women in homes struggle together to keep the pot boiling. Then why can't they study together in educational institutions?

In the modern society it is believed that the girls are not less intelligent than the boys and they have proved it. Girls are often more intelligent than the boys. They know how to tackle all the problems in a proper way. Hence if, girls and boys sit and study together they will learn a great deal of discipline, which is the most important thing in life, not only for an individual but for the whole of mankind. It is believed that the boys become gentle and civilized in the presence of girls. The girls on the other hand, learn to be frank and bold in the presence of boys.

It is also found that in co-education, both boys and girls try their best to get good marks to impress each other. Hence an inspiration of winning comes to their minds which remains a part of their whole life and proves beneficial to them in the long run.

Moreover, this system of education is economical. Education in different schools, colleges, universities, etc for both the boys and girls means double expenses. There will be two different kinds of schools, colleges and universities. This will double the number of class-rooms. There will be double the number of teachers also.

But, as we know, the world is not the same everywhere. Those who oppose this system of education give their arguments like this. They give more stress on the point of character. According to them, the co-education system spoils the character of both the boys and the girls. The boys make a show to attract the girls. Most of the boys try to look like film hero and throw their books away. Girls also become more fashionable to attract the boys and neglect their studies.

It is also found that the students sometimes start taking drugs and even commit crimes or violate the laws in order to attract the opposite sex and thus they spoil their careers.

On the whole it is better that there should be the co-education system in India. In this system, the boys and the girls can understand each other from the very beginning. Moreover, it is a fact that in the co-education system there remains less curiosity among the children about the opposite sex as they get totally mixed up.

As far as, spoiling of character is concerned, it depends upon the circle of friends and the atmosphere of one's own home. We know that the boys of colleges, schools and universities, where there is no co-education, can be seen wandering near the colleges, schools, and universities which are for girls only. It is because, the attraction between opposite sexes is a natural thing. It is for the teachers and authorities as for parents at home to keep a strict vigil. But, all the same, healthy interaction should not be disallowed.

Sometimes, a boy and a girl studying in one institution may come very close to each other. They may even go in for a matrimonial alliance later. This should not be disallowed if it is based on long, close observation and familiarity and not mere adolescent superficial attraction.

PANCHAYATI RAJ

The sturdy foundations of Indian democracy have been built with the help of Panchayati Raj institutions. The Panchayats at the village levels are the basic administrative organs of this country. The history of Panchayati Raj institutions dates back to the *Rig Vedic* times. Many ancient scriptures describe the *modus operandi* of a Panchayat System. There were established methods of elections, expulsion and inclusion of the members of the Panchayats. Panchayats were respected in the villages and their opinions and orders were implemented in letter and spirit. Even today, Panchayats remain the sole link of the governing machinery (at block or district levels) with the rural masses.

In 1815, Munro stated that if Panchayats were restrained in their operations, they could be rendered redundant. On May 15, 1989, the then Indian PM, Mr. Rajiv Gandhi, introduced a Constitutional Amendment Bill in the *Lok Sabha*. This step was taken in order to make Panchayati Raj in India an effective and a truly representative system for protecting the interests of the masses. However, the Bill could not become a law as the *Rajya Sabha* did not pass it. It was again introduced in the Parliament by the government of Mr. P.V. Narasimha Rao. It was passed as Seventy-third Constitution Amendment Act (1992) by the Indian Parliament. It came into force on April 24, 1993 and elaborates the constitution of Panchayats. It also describes the procedure of election of the chairperson of Panchayats as well as their powers. It stipulates the proportionate reservation of seats for SCs, STs and women. It also outlines the financial powers, authorities, the constitution of Finance Commission (for the purpose of reviewing their financial positions) and the powers of the State Election Commissioners.

Panchayat is elected through formal elections in a village. The elected representatives are known as *Panchas*. These *Panchas* elect a head or *Sirpancha* after mutual discussions.

The tenure of a Panchayat is 5 years. The *Panchas* and the *Sirpanch* are required to take decisions regarding the daily and routine operations of the village. A Panchayat sorts out small disputes, gives opinions about land disputes and keeps a tab on the economic and social activities of the village. The district collector and the State Judiciary depend upon the Panchayat for routine, criminal and revenue-related issues. The testimony of Panchayat or the *Panchas* in a court of law is accepted as well as respected.

There are 2.50 lakh village Panchayats, 6,022 Panchayat *Samitis* and 535 *Zila Parishads*. There are many anomalies in the operation of these institutions. However, it is in the interest of the vast Indian nation to strengthen the Panchayati Raj institutions as the operations of a nation like ours can be carried out efficiently through these institutions only. This would enable governance of our vast nation on truly democratic lives.

No other nation can claim for this unique type of governance at mass level. We have proved that we can manage each and every individual in this vast country without any tears. However, there is always a scope for improvement in this system. Reforms in Panchayati Raj institutions would ensure that justice is meted out to the needy quickly.

In sum, Panchayati Raj institutions have a bright future in India.

☆☆ *Latest Essays & Letters* ☆☆

WILDLIFE PROTECTION

While all of us are rightly so eager to manage pollution of all kinds, it is also important for us to help in protecting wildlife. We should abide by the provisions of the Wildlife Protection Act, 1972.

It is no secret that a large scale smuggling of wildlife goods is taking place all over the world in spite of requisite laws passed by a majority of countries of the world in this regard.

Elephants' ivory is sold and for that the poor elaphants are killed. Lions are killed for medicinal purposes and so are tigers. White tiger, in particular, has entered the realm of a rare species.

Another well-known rare species is the Chiru known as Tibetan Antelope (Pantholopes Hodgsoni). It is an endangered species. The famous shahtoosh shawls, priced at Rs. 1 lakh or more in the international market are made of the wool of this animal.

As per reports gathered from the press, "As the Tibetan antelope is an endangered species, there is a complete ban on the trade of goods made from the wool of Chiru in about 133 countries. Wool derived from Chiru is smuggled into India from China mostly via Leh and Ladakh especially through Darchule, Raxaul and Jaya Nagar routes. The main reason for its smuggling is that artisans are available only in Srinagar to manufacture shawls from this wool. And following manufacturing, these shawls are smuggled to countries like France and the UK where these fetch a very high price."

Under the Wildlife Protection Act, 1972, the minimum imprisonment for violation is of one year. In spite of this, every year, illegal sale of shahtoosh shawls is detected.

We must remember how our ancestors loved wildlife and sought its protection alongwith the protection of trees and forests. There are innumerable references to the wild animals in the ancient books. The Panchtantra stories are about animals. It is said that Shakuntala's son, Bharat after whose name we have named our country "Bharat" used to play with lions. Even in the medieval age, the children of Rajputs like Maharana Jashwant Singh are said to be fond of playing with lions.

Historically, we cannot forget Ashoka's lions on his piller which is our national emblem. The tiger is appropriately considered our national animal.

Let us all take a pledge to protect wildlife at all costs. It is not only because animals are also living beings like us but also because our future depends on this planet on the wildlife being safe and protected. Hence hunting of wildlife should be banned with an iron hand.

According to a report, "the centre has asked state governments to include forests and wildlife in the priority sector and come out with a five-year action plan for the protected wildlife areas on the pattern of forest working plans."

As per the report, "protected wildlife areas constitute 4.9 per cent of the country's total geographical area. This will also ensure the much needed coordination between the wildlife and the forest staff. The ministry has underlined the need for setting up special courts in the states for the effective implementation of the Wildlife Protection Act. It also proposes to amend the Act to introduce the concept of "community reserves" to recognise and ensure the people's contribution in the conservation of wildlife. A new classification of forests in the shape of special conservation areas will also be introduced to protect isolated grooves of trees."

The newspaper report further points out that "the responsibility of protecting the special conservation areas will be of the Wildlife Department. The Centre has also decided to have the same norms for the resettlement of people living within national parks and sanctuaries outside the protected areas as are applicable in case of those ousted due to the construction of big dams. The oustees will be payed a grant of Rs 1 lakh per family, besides compensation for the land lost. Taking a serious notice of the fact that officers trained in wildlife management were not being posted in the wildlife wing, the ministry has asked the states to provide details of officials trained at the Wildlife Institute of India."

TERRORISM

Of late, terrorism has become a world-wide phenomenon. India had been telling the world of the large-scale destruction being caused to life and property in Kashmir by the Pakistan sponsored terrorists. But most of the western world had turned a blind eye to India's pleadings. The west, particularly the USA, realized its taste when the (WTC) towers in America were levelled down through explosions caused by the sudden attacks by striking aeroplanes on them on 11th September, 2001 (9/11). Thus, the 9/11 event opened the eyes of the world.

As a result of this 9/11 incident, America took up the task of defending the world and getting it rid of the scourge of terrorism. Accordingly the American President in collaboration with the U.K Prime Minister drew up a road map of controlling and eliminating terrorism. A number of terrorist organisations, Al Qaeda being the most conspicuous among them, were banned. A number of countries were declared as the Axis of Evil. Afghanistan was attacked and the regime of the Taliban was brought to an end.

Later, America attacked Iraq declaring that the country possessed Weapons of Mass Destruction (WMD), although its dictatorial President Saddam Hussein denied it all along. The war was won. Later, two sons of Saddam Hussein were killed, though the President himself went underground. But, later in December 2003, he was captured in a dramatic manner in a hole under the earth and was executed in December 2006.

In Kashmir, the terrorists have been playing havoc for about two decades. Thousands of terrorists themselves, members of security forces and innocent citizens, including men and women have been killed. Indian Parliament had to face a terrorist attack on 13th December 2001. Fortunately, the Parliament which was in session was saved but a number of security guards lost their lives.

Terrorism had its heyday in Punjab in the1980s and in early 1990s. In Andhra Pradesh we have Marxist terrorists (People's War Group PWG). In Assam and some other eastern State we have ULFA, Bodo and other terrorists. In November, 2008 Mumbai was attacked by Islamic terrorists in which atleast 195 people were killed and nearly 400 injured.

In order to overcome the menace of terrorism, all the States in India and all the countries in the world should join hands to form a concerted coordinated policy.

HUMAN RIGHTS

The USA, in particular, claims to be the guardian of human rights the world over. But in USA itself President Advisory Board reported:

"Evidence presented to the board makes it clear that many whites, in general, are unaware of how colour is a disadvantage to most members of other groups."

"To understand fully the legacy of race and colour with which we are grappling, we as a nation need to understand that whites tend to benefit, either unknowingly or consciously, from this country's history of white privilege", the report stated.

Of course, there have been many violations of human rights in India as in countries like Pakistan, Bangladesh, Sri Lanka and other developing countries. Sometimes, the security forces do over-react and there is a clear violation of human rights which should not be allowed.

Certain western organisations like the Amnesty International have often taken serious view of such violations. There is the well- known Human Rights Commission in the UN also. But the point is that the terrorists also should not be allowed to violate human rights.

The human rights are very important to man. They include right to life, liberty, freedom of speech, etc. But, it has to be borne in mind that when by a particular action of an individual or organisation there is a threat to the peace and smooth working of society or when the existence or sovereignty of the state itself is jeopardised, the said human rights may be curtailed according to the law. Thus liberty is a relative term and not an absolute one and so are human rights. But whenever there is a gross violation of human rights in utter disregard of social and moral norms, the culprits must be brought to book effectively whoever they may be, whether terrorists or men in uniform, and their ill-gotten property should also be confiscated to deter them from committing such serious crimes or violations of law in future.

In India, human rights commissions have been formed at the union and state levels. All violations of such rights should be reported to these commissions. There are also National Minorities Commission & National Women's Commission. They are doing good service to the nation.

THE VALUE OF NEWS PAPERS

The two most important things in this world are the computer and the newspaper.

The newspapers give news, views, reviews and previews. Sometime the word NEWS is interpreted as North, East, West and South. It means that the newspapers provide us information and news regarding different subjects from all the directions.

The newspapers do not give just news to us. They also give us articles on all kinds of topics such as political, social, economic, monetary, business, commerce, sports, education, health, etc.

The newspapers have different columns devoted to different topics. In them we have matrimonial, editorial, readers, employment, women's, children's and other columns.

The burning problems of the day are discussed in the newspapers. Elaborate articles by experts and specialists appear in them. Then the readers' views and opinions are published in the Readers' Column which is also known as Letters to the Editor.

The newspapers are a very potent vehicle. They carry powerful advertisements which attract the attention of customers. They can make or mar a government. That is why the press is known as the Fourth Estate after the Legislature, the Judiciary and the Executive.

The newspapers also contain book-reviews of literary, historical and other books by the scholars.

Now, the newpapers are mostly in four colours. They also have weekly columns on plants, cookery, gardening, fashions, beauty concept, etc.

We must not be misled by the views expressed in newspapers. We must weigh them on the scale of reason, as some newspapers may be prejudiced. But normally newspapers are important means for spreading literacy, health-care, etc.

Let, the newspapers be objective, truthful, constructive, nationally minded, humane and with humanistic and progressive outlook.

J
EVOLUTION/SPLENDOUR OF SCIENCE

TELEVISION

Television is one of the great wonders of the modern age. It is one of the most effective means of communication to millions of people all over the world.

Television has an edge over the radio as it has a visual effect besides its sound conveyability.

At first, there was only black and white TV. Now, colour TV. is the order of the day.

Now, thanks to the satellite facilities, television has occupied its place in the houses of even, the commonest people in all parts of our country.

Now, there are numerous TV channels such as Sports Channel, News Channel, Religious Channel, etc.

Besides the Doordarshan, we have other TV companies such as Zee TV, Star TV, Jain TV etc. The cable system have come handy to the T.V. viewers. Now DTH is all poised to invade many houses.

We get news, views and entertainment over the TV. A large number of serials and films are telecast over the TV. Care should be taken that only healthy programmes are telecast.

TV is also a good means of commercial advertisement. Only good advertisements should be allowed to be telecast over the TV.

TV should be watched in a proper manner by sitting not nearer to the set than prescribed by medical authorities. Excessive viewing of TV can harm eyes, the nervous system and even independent thinking power.

THE COMPUTER

The Computer is the modern God that we have to worship. One may or may not believe in God Almighty, but one cannot disbelieve in the computer and in its utility and efficacy.

The Personal Computer (PC) is now there in many homes even in our own country. The computer has now become such a complicated thing that even perhaps Bill Gates and Premji, the great computer magnates, cannot fully explain the magnitude and extent of the present and future possibilities of the computer.

The computer can be said to be having two broad divisions the Hardware and the Software. The hardware comprises the physical components of the computer and the Software the set programme on which the computer runs.

It is said that at present India leads the world in Software and China in Hardware.

The data which is put into the computer is called the input. In the computer, the input gets changed into information. This information is treated in the computer through processing and the net result is output.

Now, the computer is being used in all kinds of technology and fields. We have electric, telephone and water bills prepared through the computer. The computer is being extensively used in banks, hotels, shops, educational institutions, hospitals, commercial and military establishments, various industries, railways, etc.

We have computerized videogames, military exercises, class notes and so many other things.

Information technology is all based on the use of the computer. It is this technology which has worked wonders for India. It has turned India from the state of a pauper to that of a wealthy and mighty nation in the making. Our space and nuclear technologies are also based on it.

MAN AND MACHINE

The modern age is the age of machines. Throughout the day and even at night, we are surrounded by the midst of machines.

We get up early in the morning on the alarm of a clock. We heat the water (in winter) with the help of the electric geyser or gas over the gas oven.

We take breakfast of pieces of bread roasted in a toaster and then we go to school or college or our place of work by bike, scooter, car or whatever vehicle we have.

If we have to travel to some place, we do so by car, bus, train, aeroplane, or ship or boat.

In the present age, there is mass production of goods in factories and mills with the help of huge machines.

If we have to visit a doctor or go to a hospital, we are confronted with several machines such as the stethoscope, the stretcher, the ECG, the EEG, the X-rays, the scanner, etc.

Most of the eatables we get such as vegetables, fruits, grains, pulses, sugar, kerosene, petrol, diesel, cooking oil, etc are carried to us in trucks, railway wagons, carts, ships, boats etc.

Even the water we drink is brought to us through taps and it may have been pumped out from the underground level with the help of machines.

Similarly, we have so many kinds of other machines. They work for us and help us. The Computer and the Robot are two of the great modern machines.

Machines save time for us. But they have to be looked after, and if they cause unemployment or excessive noise or some other inconvenience, they become a nuisance.

Still, we must remember even human body is a machine. So, machines are not altogether bad.

CINEMA

Cinema is one of the wonders of the modern world. Those who see it for the first time get thrilled and wonderstruck. The life-like presentation of people and objects is simply a triumph of science.

India is the greatest producer of films in the world. "Bollywood" has now become a byword all over the world.

Cinema has its merits as well as demerits. Used in the right manner it can bring about an awakening among the people besides providing them rich entertainment at reasonable rates. But if it is misused, it can cause great harm, particularly to the young people who are immature and are very sensitive to such things.

Unfortunately, the standard of Indian films is generally not very high. Many of them look like repeats. Moreover, they are not prepared with a moral target, but the chief aim of the producers is to earn money by playing to the gallery.

The net result is that in the films, at least in most of them, we have obscene and vulgar songs and scenes.

This is not to say that all films are bad. There are some films which are good from more than one angle. There is a Censor Board to study the films before their being released. This board should take more pains to screen all films very carefully and cut out drastically all undesirable scenes.

If the government and the producers join hands to make films a vehicle of mass awakening in various fields, there can occur a big change in the outlook of the people.

Several problems and evils such as dowry system, drug-taking, drinking, smoking, litigation, discrimination against women, dalits and backward classes can be solved to a great extent by showing healthy and well-meaning pictures. Of course, however, the recreational side of the films at the same time should not be lost sight of. It is essential to have a good story, good dialogues, good scenery, good photography, good music and songs in a film.

Only a little more contemplation and insight can help. It is good that now in many cinema houses, important matches are also shown on the big screen.

SCIENCE AND HUMAN HAPPINESS

There is no doubt that science has been the greatest boon to man so far. But the achievements of science have not come to man as a ripe apple falls in the lap of a man sitting under an apple tree. Science is not just the result of observation and experience. It is, on the other hand, the result of centuries of hard work done by man, even at the risk of his own life or health.

Today, man can fly in space. He can fly in the air like birds. He can swim on the surface of the sea like fishes. He can move on the earth at tremendous speed. More recently, he can keep sitting at home and do tele-shopping. He can chat and learn a lot on the Internet and also express his own viewpoint through e-mail.

If some outstanding scientific achievements of the twentieth century are to be mentioned, the discovery of electricity must perhaps come at the top. The electricity brings in its train innumerable devices like the fluorescent tube, the bulb, the fan, the desert cooler, the air-conditioner, the geyser etc. Even the printing presses, textile and hundreds of other mills and factories and the cinematographs and computers and T.V. sets and the radio also work with electricity though the battery cells may also be used in some cases.

The most notable achievements of science are in the fields of agriculture, industry and medicine and surgery.

In the fields of medicine and surgery, literally miraculous progress has been done. What are these—the bypass surgery, ballooning, heart and kidney and bone-marrow transplant? They are nothing short of miracles.

Today, the people are greatly health conscious. Longevity has increased in most of the countries. Child mortality has been greatly reduced in number. We have so many health centres, gyms and slimming centres and nursing homes, hospitals and maternity centres.

In the field of education and dissemination of knowledge, we have the use of e-mail, e-class-rooms, better schools, new teaching and learning methods, study through cassettes and several video-audio methods.

In fact man is still exploring the vast uncharted vistas on the earth and in the sky. He is still trying to probe deeply into the past. Let us hope for the best.

MOBILE TECHNOLOGY

Now a day's every individual use the mobile technology. In 1946 first telephone call was made and in 1965 first cordless phone was invented.

After that AT&T launched the IMTS in 1971. First commercial call is made in the year of 1983.

From the year of 1946, mobile technology encountered lot of changes. The invention of the Bluetooth is made in the year of 1994 and the first camera image is taken in the year of 1997. In the year of 2001 first 3G service is launched. These are the important milestone of mobile technology.

Cellular communication uses the mobile technology. In past few years CDMA technology improved rapidly. Mobile technology is based on mobility of devices. Such technology is used in various industries like car etc.

Mobile technology is specially used by mobile phones for wireless communication purposes. Transferring of data done through mobile technology by means of voice, text, videos, images etc. Mobile technology provides the portability of devices. Example of portable devices is: • Laptop • Mobile phones • GPS devices • Tablets. Mobile technology provides the improved services to users and provides the flexibility in work.

Mobile computing allows people to use IT without being tied to a single location. Any business with staff that works away from the office can benefit from using it. Whether you are travelling to meetings, out on sales calls, working from a client's site or from home, mobile devices can help you keep in touch and make the most productive use of your time. You can use a range of devices to stay in touch including laptops, notebooks, personal digital assistants and 'third generation' (3G) smart phones. Mobile IT devices can also change the way you do business. New technologies lead to new ways of working and new products and services that can be offered to your customers. Mobile technology is exactly what the name implies—technology that is portable.

SCIENCE AND RELIGION

Science and religion seem to be antagonistic to each other. But intrinsically, their purpose is the same—that is, to make life happy and worth living. Both claim to be based on truth, though their methods are different.

There are many similarities and dissimilarities between science and religion. The basis of science in earliest stages at least, is believed to have been observation and experience, and it is quite understandable that man must have been observing the natural phenomena and having some experiences of varied type. Yet, religion is believed to be much older than science. It is because religion is primarily based on belief and faith which later took the shape of magic. But science in its tangible form came to be recognized much later.

It is now almost established that man has evolved from other species after the passage of numerous milleniums. As he appeared on the earth in the present human form, he was awed to watch the lightning in the sky followed by a loud thunder. As he moved on the earth, he came across or experienced floods and forest fires which made him realize the presence of some spirit behind all such things and happenings. He began to feel and realize and associate his own life and fate in the hands of some invisible power whom perhaps he gave the name of God. The fact that the name of God in different vernaculars, languages and dialects exists almost all over the world in all religions, among all races and countries, means that either all mankind was thinking alike at one or the other time or the people in different regions or areas of the world were having some communication system even unconsciously, may be in the form of conveying of some fact, information, secret or piece of knowledge from person to person through the mouth, as the writing process, as we know now, came much later, indeed, recently only.

Whatever might be the origin of science and religion, the main point is their area of activity and their method of working.

Science makes a man rational and free-minded. Religion wants man to believe blindly in what he is told to be true and worthy of being practised. Science asks questions and puts every thesis or proposal to test. Religion abhors such methods.

Science believes in logical experiments and wants to declare something truthful and true if it comes out finally resultant of the experiment. Religion pre-supposes the result and wants to stick to it irrespective of the outcome of investigation, inquiry or experiment.

So, religion and science both are complementary to each other. For mankind, both are required in equal measure and simultaneously. Thus intrinsically, both are essential for man.

MEANS OF COMMUNICATION

To communicate means to contact somebody or some people mostly for some purpose just as business, discussion of a matter or problem or for conveying a message, etc.

We can divide communication into two kinds—personal communication and mass communication.

The means of personal communication are postal letters, parcels, packets etc., courier services, telephones, telegrams, fax, e-mail, or internet, etc.

If we want to communicate or interact with a person in brief, we can make use of the telegram or the telephone or the pager. But if we have to send a lengthy message or material to somebody, we can make use of a letter, a packet or a parcel sent through post or courier service, fax or e-mail, etc. Now, sometimes, even personal messages are conveyed through certain columns in newspapers or certain serials run by the T.V. managements or administrators. Normally, newspapers and T.V. can be regarded only as means of mass communication.

Mass communication is possible through newspapers, T.V., cinema, e-mail, internet, radio, etc.

Mass communication can mean message to a specific section of society or a large segment of populace.

In the newspapers we have news, advertisements of various kinds and material on sports, education, health, gardening, books, employment, etc. There are certain things for mass programme, such as awareness regarding AIDS, Hepatitis, Polio, etc. Invitations to attend an inauguration by a dignitary should also come under this category.

Cinema, T.V., radio, newspapers, etc. can also be used as great vehicles of social change besides their entertaining and education value.

Strictly speaking, books should be considered as one of the important means of mass communication, as they carry the messages of scholars and experts in various fields not only to the present generation but also to the coming generations.

SCIENCE - AND ITS BLISSFUL ASPECTS

Science has changed human life altogether. The fabrics that we wear are manufactured in the factories. The machines that we use in every day life, are manufactured in most parts of the world. The cookers, the coolers, the refrigerators, radio-sets, television-sets, cameras, telephones, wireless systems, telescopes, microscopes and other such instruments have become sources of human comfort. Man may converse with his friends and relatives living thousands of miles away. We have seen the pictures of the planets reach our earth through space by electronically-fitted cameras. A man sitting on earth may see the surface of the mars millions of miles away in space.

The buses, ships, aeroplanes, scooters and even bicycles have minimised distance to a greater extent. To reach New York from Delhi is a matter of hours.

We know of the vast caravans of traders trekking their way through the deserts of Rajasthan and Iran to the distant places such as Greece and Turkey in medieval times. People used to walk or ride the beasts of burden upto thousands of miles to sell their goods. There were boats, but today there are ships of the modern size that bring thousands of tonnes of goods to various countries easily. Science has placed at our disposal a vast variety of experimental knowledge. In big laboratories, experiments are conducted on many subjects and thus research goes on unabated. Our country also has got many research laboratories. On one side, research is being conducted for benefiting humanity and on the other hand, atomic weapons being piled up by the super powers for fighting future wars.

There are missiles having nuclear war-heads and other bombs that may destroy big cities in a matter of minutes. Hiroshima and Nagasaki in Japan were destroyed in a matter of minutes when atomic bombs were dropped in those cities at the end of the second World War in 1945. But now the people are aware of the dangers posed by nuclear weapons and efforts are being made by the UN and other bodies to stop the nuclear race.

India wants peace in the world and wishes that every country should destroy the atomic weapons or at least call a halt to it forthwith.

Thus, man is progressing by manufacturing good things of life and at the same time he is making progress in manufacturing atomic and space weapons to destroy the human race.

Again this is not all. People have become more money minded. They are not like their forefathers who were simple and religious. They treated God as the Almighty. They feared God. But the modern man has almost forgotten those values of life.

Science has changed human outlook to a great extent. He is not a carefree man like his ancestors. He leads an artificial way of life. He glorifies in outward comforts of life. Thus science has dealt a blow to the ancient values of humanity.

If the man starts thinking of the future of the human race, he must have to give up the path of destruction. If he works like a sane man and stops working for building up nuclear arsenals, this earth is bound to turn into a heaven, otherwise the worst type of disaster may wipe out the remains of human and other types of life on this beautiful-planet. Science is a blessing in disguise, but if the scientific knowledge is misused, it makes hell of it.

INTERNET

Internet is the logical conglomeration of computer systems that are spread around the world. It has been created with the help of optical cable networks, modern devices, telephone lines, LAN and WAN networks and satellites. Information is displayed on various web sites on the Internet. This information is related to almost every area of human endeavour, including environment, space and facts related to the cosmos.

In the Internet jargon, if a person opens the Internet web sites on his computer (or surfs through the web sites), then he is called Netizen. Presently, there are nearly 42.9 crore Internet connections in India. Internet is a boon for a nation like India. It helps us exchange vital information and data and our readers know that in the present information technology age, information is everything. Almost all the governments of the world, private firms, non-government organisation and professionals either want to get their web sites developed or surf through various Internet web sites. Many of them have got their web sites developed and also got them uploaded on this wonderful information superhighway. Not only this, there are web sites of many newspapers, magazines and technical journals as well.

This method of information exchange is very efficient and fast. E-mail can be used by Netizens to send information to any part of the world. Voice, data, video information and information in the form of text can be sent from one computer to another with ease. Besides, Internet has put man on the peak of the business world. This concept is called Electronic Commerce (E-com). Electronic Commerce is related to the exchange of goods and services through the Net and in this system, money is not physically transferred. It is transferred through a new system, which is called Electronic Cash (E-cash). We can buy and sell practically anything through Internet; exchange of data for engineering projects is also included in this system

There are three levels of connectivity of Internet. The first level is T1 in which, the user can only see the information/data put on various web sites. The second level is T2 in which, he can create his own web sites as well as collect information from the Net. The third level is T3 in which, he himself becomes a part of the Internet System. Nowadays, VSNL, Mantra Online and Satyam Online are the three major Internet Service Providers (ISPs). Many other firms are entering the vast markets related to Internet services. VSNL has been privatised now. Internet affects all the areas of human endeavour. It has been successful in earning valuable achievements in fields like education, entertainment, sports and games, science and technology, Electronic Commerce and social interactions (like marriage alliances). This world has already taken the shape of a small village. The government has provided local dial-up service in all the districts of the country. A user, who is located within the 100-kilometer radius of an ISP, can use Internet services through a local telephone line. In order to surf through Internet, we have to connect our computer system to the main information gateway of the ISP through a telephone line and modem. We use Internet navigation software to surf through Internet. These programs are provided by Microsoft Corporation (Internet Explorer) or Netscape (Netscape Navigator). Dialling is automatic over the telephone and if a connection is made, then we arrive at the main menu of the ISP. We can surf through any web site if we feed its correct URL on the computer's screen at the command line. We can surf through various web sites, send and receive E-mail, read magazines and even listen to music.

There is also a lot of garbage-like information on the Net, which is related to obscene photographs and movies. It is sad to note that the youth of today do not use Internet for educational purposes, or for enhancing their professional capabilities. This tendency ought to be given a U-turn.

In sum, Internet would become a dominant force in the areas related to professional, social, business and entertainment activities of all the people in this century.

❏ ❏ ❏

K
PLACES OF REPUTE/
HERITAGE/MONUMENT

TAJMAHAL OF AGRA

The Taj Mahal is one of the most famous historical buildings of India. It was built in 17th century by the Mughal Emperor Shah Jehan in the memory of his beloved wife, Mumtaz Mahal.

The Taj is situated on the banks of the sacred river, Yamuna. It is made of pure white marble. It is said that more than twenty thousand masons and artisans built it in more than twenty years. It lies at Agra in Uttar Pradesh.

Last Sunday, I with my brother went to see the Taj. It was a full moon night. I had rightly heard that the mausoleum is a sight to see on a full moon-night. I was completely enthralled as it present a magical look.

First, we reached the red gateway. We walked on a passage flanked by rows of symmetrical, beautiful cypress trees on either side, which bordered spacious lush green lawns. At the very first sight of the mausoleum I felt as if I had fallen in love with it.

One of the most impressive structural charm was because of the tall spiral minarets emerging from the four corners of the building. The dome itself is beggars description.

I saw carved birds and flowers in marble besides hymns from the holy Koran. I also visited the tombs of Shah Jehan and his wife, Mumtaz Mahal.

After staying there for some time I left the place half-heartedly. I'm, indeed, so enchanted with the beauty of the Taj that I have decided to visit the monument during each summer vacation.

The Taj Mahal is one of the seven wonders of the world and people from all over the world visit Agra to see its splendour and beauty.

DELHI : OUR CAPITAL

Delhi is the Capital of our country. Delhi is a very old city founded in the 11th century A.D. by a Rajput chieftain of the Tomar clan. In 1912, the Capital of British India was transferred from Calcutta to Delhi. New Delhi was built much later. But they are joined and practically form one city which is called Delhi. So, although all the important offices concerning the reins of government ruling the country lie in New Delhi, in general, Delhi is known as the Capital of India which includes New Delhi also.

The head of the Indian State is the President. He lives in the Rashtrapati Bhawan in Delhi. The Prime Minister who is the elected head of the Government of India also resides in Delhi. The Parliament which is the law-making body for the country, is also situated in Delhi. The Supreme Court is the highest court in the country and it is also situated in Delhi.

Delhi has a mammoth population which is more than 16.7 million. Thousands of people come here daily from neighbouring states for employment purposes.

In Delhi there are several buildings worth-seeing, such as the Red Fort, the Qutub Minar, the Jantar Mantar, the Connaught Place, the India Gate, the Jama Masjid, the Lotus Temple, the Humayun Tomb, etc., besides the Parliament House and the Rashtrapati Bhawan already mentioned.

Delhi is a city of parks, museums, art gallaries, libraries, schools, colleges and universities.

Several fairs are held here at the Pragati Maidan Exhibition Ground. There is an efficient bus system in Delhi. Now, the Metro Rail System has also been introduced. Today, New Delhi is extending imposing dimensions, i.e., modern building, both residential and official, broad, well planned roads and fly-overs, that make New delhi a truly beautiful city.

Previously, Delhi was highly polluted. Now, the problem has been solved to a great extent by the shifting of factories out of Delhi and the introduction of gas instead of petrol and diesel for vehicles.

A Visit To A Hill Station

During summer, plains get awfully hot. So, everybody wants to escape from this heat. No doubt, some people have ACs or desert coolers in their houses. But these man-made gadgets are no match for natural coolness which is available at the hills.

Every year, I visit one or the other hill station during summer. Last summer, I went to Shimla.

I caught a bus from Chandigarh. The bus passed through many tunnels which were quite dark and awesome.

As the bus reached the outskirts of Shimla, all the passengers in the bus began to appreciate being welcomed by wafts of cool, soothing breeze.

From the Shimla bus stand, I left straight for my uncle's house. My uncle is a forest officer at Shimla.

I was welcomed by my aunt as I went there without any prior intimation. My aunt phoned my uncle at once and he arrived within a few minutes. He was very glad to see me.

The next day, my uncle took me in his jeep. We passed through a dense forest of pine trees. The leaves of the trees were wavering in the wind and birds sitting in them were singing sweet songs. We also saw many gurgling rivulets and springs. He asked me to look at the snowcapped mountain peaks which were situated at some distance. We also saw a number of wild animals like deer, jackals, foxes, rabbits and others in the forest. We also visited the Jakhoo Temple.

What exhilarated me most was the frequent drizzling. In fact, clouds were almost always present in the sky.

I lived at Shimla for about a month. I had daily morning walks and exercise. I greatly gained in health. As I returned home, my mother was in particular, very happy as she saw that I had, after all, become a fine figure.

A Visit To The Zoo

Last Sunday, I went to the zoo alongwith my uncle. We bought the tickets at the main gate and went inside.

The first thing which pleased me most was the purity and freshness of air. The sight of beautiful green trees and plants was also quite exhilarating.

As we went a little further, we saw a big lake like tank. I was greatly amused when I saw ducks, swans and other water birds swimming in water. Some of them were sitting on the banks and preening their feathers.

We proceeded further, I saw a huge crowd of children and adults at some distance. As I saw carefully, I noticed a large number of monkeys and apes jumping from branch to branch. They were gibbering and staring at the onlookers.

Some children were throwing peanuts and parched grams towards the monkeys. The latter picked up the grams and peanuts and ate them leisurely. My uncle had also brought those things with him. He gave me a handful of them. I also threw them towards the monkeys. As the naughty animals picked them up I felt very happy. I also felt amused when I found some monkeys imitating the gestures of the grown-ups.

We moved forward. In a cage we saw a lion. It was roaring. Some children were teasing it. It was very bad on their part. Moreover, a worker in the zoo told us that it was dangerous to poke ones finger or hand inside a lion's cage.

We also saw many other animals such as wolves, bears, hyenas, deer, foxes, jackals and sparrows of many colours. The birds that pleased me most were ostrich, penguin and kiwi.

In the end, I had an elephant ride. It was the grand finale to our visit which I'll never forget.

THE QUTUB MINAR

The Qutub Minar stands proud and erect as one of India's rich heritages. This is yet another beautiful monument which takes us back to the past. The intricate structure, and designs carved painstakingly by our skilled craftsmen, tell of monuments and buildings made by Kings and Nawabs of bygone days.

The Qutub Minar in Delhi is one such structure. It was begun first by Qutub-ud-Din Aibak, from where it got its name, in AD 1200, but was completed by the Iltutmish who succeeded him, as Aibak was not able to do so. It is situated in South Delhi near Mehrauli. The pillar stands 242 feet high. Built originally with seven storeys, its height stretched to about 300 feet. It is a compact Octagonal building of red sandstone, crowned by a beautiful white marble dome. The sandstone used at the base of the monument matches the dark orange coloured stone used in the 5th storey.

The three-tower storeys have bands of Arabic writting on them. The plinth is a polygon of 20 sides. A balcony runs round each storey. Almost eight centuries have gone by since it was made, yet, it stands firm and strong. People throng to see it from all parts of the world for it has great tourist appeal.

A VISIT TO A MUSEUM

There are many museums all over the world. Numerous museum are there in India itself. Most of the museums are specific and have items pertaining to a particular field or area. Such are Railway Museum, Air Force Museum, Doll Museum, Statue Museum and so on.

Last Sunday, I went to see the museum pertaining to the Archaeological Survey of India. It comprised a number of rooms. Each room showed items concerning a particular period in the history of India or pertaining to a particular region of India.

The most impressive items that virtually enthralled me were the items pertaining to the Harappa and Mohenjodaro Civilization. Models and real findings from this civilization were displayed in elaborate showcases. Besides, there were charts, pictures and posters depicting disparate items.

I was greatly impressed by the model of the Great Bath and the wonderful drainage system in the ancient urban civilization. Then I looked at toys of animals, men and birds with great curiosity. I also had a glance at the mysterious script of the language of the Harappans.

Some other things which had a great effect on my mind were the coins, utensils, toys etc. of different periods in India's history such as the Chola period, the Maurya period, the Gupta period, the Tughlaq period, the Mughal period, etc.

I saw many other things and when I returned home after about two hours, I was full of new knowledge and somewhat whetted hunger for attaining more of it elsewhere.

A VISIT TO AN EXHIBITION

The exhibition is the showing or displaying of some art or specified set of items. Now-a-days, painters have to display their paintings to bring them to the notice of the people. In fact, book fairs, film festivals, music concerts, beauty contests, are practically all a kind of exhibition.

The most elaborate exhibitions in Delhi are held in the exhibition ground of the Pragati Maidan on the Mathura Road.

Last week, I got an opportunity to visit a Science Exhibition which was being held in the exhibition ground.

The exhibition was a feast to the mind as it offered a plethora of new knowledge in various scientific fields.

There were numerous posters hanging on the walls. These posters contained maps, charts, pictures, diagrams, tables and statements and research reports, in a nutshell, of various scientific research scholars.

I learnt a lot about different kinds of bacteria and about development and remedies concerning various diseases.

The engineering feats of India and other countries were also displayed. There were several machines, devices and gadgets which I had not heard or seen before.

India's progress in the field of Information Technology was also well highlighted.

As I returned home, I found myself too stuffed with knowledge to help boasting about my visit to the wonderland.

❏❏❏

MISCELLANEOUS (STUDENT'S CONCERN)

OUR SCHOOL LIBRARY

Our school library is situated in a corner of the school. It is a big library.

Our school library comprises two big halls for books, one room for the librarian and his officials, one room for staff and a big reading room for students.

There are more than fifty thousand books in our school library. There are books on all subjects. Apart from the books concerning subjects taught in the school, there are books on other subjects such as sports, magic, astronomy, astrology, psychology, horticulture, poultry, handicrafts, bee-keeping, etc.

Our school librarian is a middle-aged man. His name is Manohar Lal. He is an M.A. M.Lib. He is a very learned man and has mastery over a number of subjects. He keeps studying books during his spare time. He is very gentle and polite. The officials working under him are also very good-natured persons.

The catalogue of books bearing the title, the author's name, publisher's name, subject and other particulars are kept in a big chest comprising many card boxes kept in pigeon-holes. Each book has been allotted a card and bears a distinct number. Thus, it is not difficult to locate a book. In case of any difficulty, the librarian and his subordinates assist the students.

A student can get one book at a time. He can keep it for a fortnight. Thereafter, he can get the period of the book extended for one week and in case there is no demand from any other student or member of the staff for the book, he can get it extended further.

If a student keeps a book for a period which is more than the prescribed period, he has to pay a penalty of one rupee per day.

There are separate rows of tall shelves in which books are kept. The shelves are arranged subject-wise.

The library also contributes to several journals and magazines in various languages and on various-subjects.

I am, indeed, proud of my school library.

MY BEST FRIEND

I have many friends. All friends cannot be termed as best or even good. Most of them are selfish and opportunists.

My best friend is Krishnamurthy. He is of my age. He studies in my class. He is my next door neighbour. We go to school together. We sit on the same bench. We also do our homework together.

Krishnamurthy is a very intelligent boy. He always stands first in the class. He is among the best students of the class. He is also a good player of hockey. He takes a keen interest in co-curricular activities.

He also takes care of his health. He gets up early in the morning and goes out for a walk. He takes some exercise in park and comes back home with energy replenished.

However, it is a not just for these qualities that I love Krishnamurthy. It is not only because of these things that I consider him a great human being and trust him.

He has a high moral character. He never tells a lie. He is a boy of his word. He stands by me through thick and thin. He helps me whenever I'm in need of his help. He is a boy of sincerity and integrity. Even our teachers acknowledge his high sense of truth and honesty at such a tender stage.

Krishnamurthy is also a brave boy. Only last week he saved a drowning child while putting his own life at risk. Last year, he saved a child who was inadvertently left in a burning house by his parents.

Once we were having a trekking expedition in the Himalayas. Suddenly, my foot slipped and I fell down. I got a fracture in my leg. It was Krishnamurthy who took me to hospital and remained with me till

I recovered. He incurred all my medical expenses from his own pocket and refused to accept them when I offered him money.

I'm proud of such a friend. Truly, Krishnamurthy is my best friend. May he live long!

My Hobby

Everybody must have one or many hobbies. It is particularly important after doing some strenuous physical or intellectual work.

One can have more than one hobbies. But usually people have just one hobby and that is enough.

A hobby should not be carried too far such as to devote more time on it than on your main work.

My hobby is gardening, I spend my whole Sunday or other holiday on this hobby.

I fetch good seeds or saplings of various plants from a standard nursery and grow them in my kitchen garden.

In my kitchen garden, I have flower and fruit plants, in particular. I also grow some vegetables there according to the season.

Among the flowers, which I like most are Roses, Daffodils, Jasmines, Lilies, and Sunflowers.

The vegetables that I generally grow there are Cauliflower, Cabbage, Spinach, Lady's finger, Pumpkin, etc.

There are also a few fruit trees in my kitchen garden. Particularly worth mentioning are Guava, Pomegranate, Mulberry, Blackberry, Litchi, Chikoo etc.

I water the plants regularly. I take out weeds from the beds. I also apply the required quantity of manure regularly.

When some of the plants bear fruit, I have to be very wary of the predatory birds such as parrots. Such plants as guavas and papayas have particularly to be taken care of.

Sometimes, I have also to apply some insecticides and pesticides in small quantities.

I am proud of my hobby. It gives me light exercise, recreation and happiness and good vegetables, flowers and some fruit.

A FAREWELL PARTY AT SCHOOL

My last day at school was a memorable one. It was in time with the long tradition of the school according to which the outgoing students are given a farewell party to the students of the class next to their class.

When I was in the XI class, we had given a farewell party to the students of class XII who were about to leave the school to appear in the Board Examination.

Now, I was in the XII class and our Board examination was to start in March. The school was going on preparatory holidays from 26th February. So, the farewell party to our class was given by the students of the XI class on 25th February which was the last working day of the session.

The XI class students did a lot of homework to make the day a memorable one. They took great pains to decorate the school hall with balloons and bunting. They themselves fixed the chairs, sofas and carpets.

Our school Principal presided over the function. Beside him sat other teachers on the sofas and chairs on the stage.

A cultural programme comprising songs, skits, folk dances and short speeches was held. In the speeches which were made by teachers and students, some very touching words were spoken.

We had been invited by the XI class students through small artistic invitation cards. Light refreshments were served to all.

We in our speeches for their love shown to us as well as the hospitality extended to us.

In our speeches, we also begged pardon of the teachers, if we had ever disobeyed them or misbehaved with any of them.

In the end, the Principal made a short speech, exhorting us and explaining the importance of studies. He assured us that there was no necessity for begging pardon of the teachers as they had no ill-will in their mind. Whatever they did or had said to us was only for our well-being.

We realized that the teachers were really our well-wishers and our representative amply expressed his gratitude to them.

We went home happily even while missing our teachers, friends in other classes and school itself. We were full of zeal and self-confidence.

Our National Flag

National flag is the symbol of a country's freedom and sovereignty. It is the flag under which our freedom fighters had fought for India's Independence.

Before Independence, the National Flag had the spinning wheel placed at its centre. It was necessary at that time to do so to remind the people of the Swadeshi Movement started by Gandhiji along with the movement for freedom.

After Independence, the spinning wheel was replaced by the Ashok Chakra. The Ashok Chakra has 24 spokes. It stands for peace and love which enshrined the state of the famous emperor, Ashoka.

Our National flag is rectangular in shape. It has three horizontal bands. Each band is of a different colour. That is why the flag is also called the Tricolour or the *Tiranga*.

At the top is the saffron band which symbolises the spirit of sacrifice. The middle band is the white band which characterizes peace and truth. It is in this band that the peace-spreading Ashoka Chakra is located, thus enhancing the significance of peace and love. At the bottom is the dark green band which stands for growth and prosperity.

The National flag is hoisted on important buildings on national festivals. Now, the Supreme Court has given enough liberty to the people to fly the National flag. But, all rules according to the relevant Act governing its hoisting, have to be followed. On the death of some celebrity, it flies half-mast over buildings.

It is imperative for us to respect our national flag and never let it down. We should be ready to lay down our life for its high position that it deserves.

My Ambition In Life

In the modern world nobody can live without doing one or the other profession. The days of non-doing hermits, monks and nuns are long over.

I'm studying in one of the best public school in the state. My aim is to gain as much knowledge about different subjects as I can.

As I'm still a young student, it is not very easy for me to say categorically what I want to be in life.

In spite of this, something can be said, keeping in view my aptitude and circumstances and financial position and views of my parents.

My father is an army officer and for that reason I have learnt that discipline and patriotism are the two great virtues in life.

However, mere possession of these virtues is not enough. There is a hard competition ahead. I must get through the NDA and other relevant examinations and get a high position in them. All that is easier said than done.

I'm working hard. My parents find no difficulty in procuring for me all the necessary books and coaching facilities. My father himself is a beacon-light for me. He not only guides me but also inspires me, and that is why I'm so full of confidence.

I'm a brilliant student at school and I hope I'll remain so all my life. I do not think I need to be humble beyond the proper limit. Hence, I've no hesitation in saying that I want to be an army officer and I'm confident that I'll successfully achieve my aim and ambition.

MY CLASS TEACHER

Mr. Pramod Bhandari is my class teacher. He is a first rate teacher. He teaches us English.

He is a middle-aged respectable, well-dressed, slim man with polished manners. He is very simple and polite and has an attractive personality.

Mr. Bhandari comes of a noble family, but he loves people of all castes and religions. He says that his true Goddess is Mother India and his religion is patriotism. At the same time, he says, that we should not hate the people of other countries. In fact, we should love all mankind.

Mr. Bhandari has a mastery over his subject. He is an M.A., B.Ed. He speaks English fluently. His range of vocabulary sometimes surprises. He is full of new constructive ideas. He understands all the subtle intricacies of grammar very well. But he does not teach the students beyond their heads. His way of teaching is very interesting. He explains everything thoroughly. He never bores the class.

Mr. Bhandari never gets impatient with the students. He does not beat any student. He does not give severe punishment even to the naughtiest students in the class. He does rebuke them, often politely and rarely strongly, but they know that he does not do so for vengeance or on prestige issue. They know that he is their true well-wisher.

All the students love him. He is in the good books of the Principal who often praises him for his sincerity and industriousness. He takes extra classes of weak students free of charge. He wants them to make up their deficiency. He tries his best to make them do so.

I not only love him but also adore him. May he live long!

ANNUAL PRIZE DISTRIBUTION FUNCTION

The annual prize distribution function of our school was held last Sunday. The President of the local Municipal Committee, Mr. P.K. Mathur presided over the function.

The function was held in the school playground. The place was tastefully decorated with balloons and bunting a day earlier.

The whole place looked like a heaven of colour, enthusiasm and merriment.

The Chief guests arrived in time. He was taken to the 'Pandal' by the Principal and the Vice-Principal.

The Chief guest was given a standing ovation. Then the cultural programme started. There were songs, qawwalis, skits, hymns, folk dances and speeches. A brief debate on "How to Improve the Education System" was also organised. My friend, Mohit, was declared the best speaker. Later, he was also given a prize alongwith others.

After the cultural programme, the Prize Distribution Function was held. The students who excelled in various fields such as studies, sports, painting, singing and other co-curricular activities during the year, were given prizes by the Chief Guest.

The sportspersons were not given prizes at this function, as the Annual sports meet had already been held and these persons had already been honoured.

After the function, the Principal made a short speech highlighting the achievements of the school during the year. Later, the chief guest made a brief speech praising the good results of the school in various fields during the year.

The function came to an end after the chanting of the National Anthem.

TOURISM

Tourism has turned out to be a very important industry in the modern age. In almost all the countries of the world there are separate ministries of tourism.

Tourist spots are being developed all over the world to attract the tourists. Tourism is, indeed, a good source of earning foreign exchange for every country that can manage it efficiently.

All over the world there is a great interaction between people of different countries, races, communities, regions and religions. Business magnates visit other countries to promote their business.

Writers, also move about in different countries and at different spots in search of new themes and to gain knowledge about men and objects they want to write about.

Several newspaper agencies, journalists, scribes, radio and T.V. reporters and others connected with mass media have to roam from place to place to trace out essential and interesting matter for reporting purposes.

Most of the tourists, however, are in search of entertainment, exploration and adventure, alongwith which they also want to enhance their knowledge in various fields.

Such men and women have to stay in hotels and they often stay in good hotels—five star or others. They are ready to pay adequately for the good food, lodging, comfort given and entertainment provided.

Many tourists visit tourist spots such as beaches, hill stations, historical and picturesque places, religious and cultural programmes and congregations.

Tourists are also fond of participating in adventure games and swimming bouts and visiting Sanctuaries of animals and birds and zoos, museums, exhibitions, etc.

THE VALUE OF TIME

It is often said that punctuality is the courtesy of kings. We should, however, remember that time is a highly precious thing.

We have only a limited time period in life in which we are to act and grow and find fulfilment. If we waste this golden opportunity, we are no better than fools of the first water.

A student who does not care for time, actually attracts the conclusion that time need not care for him, and time actually doesn't care for such a sluggard and shirker. Time marches on leaving behind all the lazy, sluggish lot who turns into worthless straws in the race of life.

Such a student as does not get up early in the morning, cannot go to school or college in time and pay full attention to his studies. Hence he fails not only in his examination but also in life.

A farmer who does not sow seeds and water the plants at the proper time, should hope to get no crops at the end of the season.

An army that does not reach the battlefield at the right time, loses the battle.

A businessman who does not catch an opportunity for the progress or maintenance of his business, may lose even his capital in the long run.

There is no doubt that several litterateurs, philosophers, thinkers and ideologists have spoken strongly against modern man's excessive obsession with time. They may be right in their own way. It is true that the stress and strain and sick hurry of modern life are by and large responsible for so many ailments and diseases such as hypertension, heart attack, paralysis etc.

Be it as it may, the fact remains that when we have been cast in this world, we have to work and act according to circumstances. The situation is such that we cannot help acting quickly and wisely. Every moment lost may be worth more than a dollar.

Everything is marching towards death and decay. Our life is short. We must act quickly and gain all the knowledge and enjoy ourselves as much as we can in this short period.

For enjoyment, we need money and money cannot be had except through work. Hence we must work and work meticulously.

We must do everything in a well-planned manner, dividing every unit of time to take full advantage of it.

As for tension, stress and strain, we should channelise other methods such as meditation, yoga, exercise, pursuit of some hobby, etc. for a limited period and that at regular intervals.

If we manage our time properly, we can get prosperity, enjoyment of luxuries, peace of mind, indeed, everything. Otherwise, we lose everything.

It depends on all of us what we want to choose.

OUR EDUCATION SYSTEM

During the British period, the System of education was devised by the rulers as per their own convenience.

After Independence, it was realized that this education system must be overhauled for the benefit of the masses of this country.

Several Education Commissions and Committees were established and several experiments in the field of education were made.

Finally, the 10 + 2 + 3 system of education was accepted as a model system.

The system has been put to trial almost all over the country and it seems to have stood the test of time.

According to this system, there is high school teaching upto class X. It covers ten years.

After the 10th class, there is two year teaching (+2) in a school or college (generally a school).

After this, there is teaching for three years in a university for the student to get a degree. The first ten years school teaching and thereafter 2 year teaching are controlled by a Senior Secondary School Education Board.

According to this system, the student studies a number of arts and science subjects at school which are compulsory for all students. Thereafter, he studies some subjects of his choice arts/science/commerce etc.

Thereafter, the student may join some professional or vocational course according to his aptitude and calibre. The brilliant ones interested in higher studies may join a university for three years to do graduation.

The system seems to have worked well though it deserves some improvement in a number of ways.

THE SECRET OF SUCCESS

It is common to say : "Nothing succeeds like success." The meaning of this saying is that success comes to man not by means of his own efforts but by chance. In other words, in the matter of succeess, man is a slave in the hands of chance and circumstances.

This view, however, is erroneous, as it is not based on reality. There is no doubt that there are some people who get success even beyond their wildest dreams. Sometimes, a man gets success when actually he thinks that he is going to fail.

In most of the cases in real life, we find that there are some solid factors behind the lives of all successful men who are in the present world known as achievers.

Among such factors we can categorize hard work, acumen, shrewdness, meticulous-planning, proper and timely guidance, goodness and taking of certain risk. It is necessary that a person who wants to get success in any venture, should be well-equipped for it. He must have proper aptitude for it. He must have a strong determination to fulfil his ambition. He must have patience and the virtue of stubborn perseverance and commitment. His ambition and ideal must be lofty. He must be a man of principle, integrity and sincerity such that others can easily repose faith in him. He must have the proper talents which are necessary for the execution of the project in hand.

It is of utmost importance that one must have the qualities of leadership, mutual trust, cooperation, team-spirit and friendship.

Above all, one must have a positive attitude. One must be bubbling with optimism, hope and enthusiasm. A pessimistic person with a negative attitude towards life can achieve nothing. One must have first succeeded in one's mind before achieving success in the field. Minor obstacles should not flag one's spirit.

MY COUNTRY

India is my country and I am proud of it. I believe in letter and spirit what Sir Walter Scott, a famous poet and novelist has said about one's native land:

"Breathes there the man with soul so dead,

Who never to himself has said,

'This is my own, my native land?"

Scott believes that such a man just cannot exist.

Even a small sparrow living in a small nest, loving dearly its young ones, loves the nest more than its own life. Then why should man be less than even a sparrow? It will be the height of ingratitude on the part of a man not to love his country, his native land.

Many people in the world believe in the dictum: "My country, right or wrong." But extreme nationalism leads to chauvinism which is harmful to the interests of mankind. We should try to be nationalists as well as internationalists like Gandhi and Tagore. In the modern world, of course, the geographical boundaries are fast disappearing as more and more men and women are emerging as citizens of the world.

Even from India, many people have emigrated to countries such as America, England, Australia, New Zealand, Italy, Canada, etc. Many of them hold green cards and others have obtained citizenship there.

Even the Non-resident Indians (NRIs) love India, at least, most of them.

India is a vast country. Even in the matter of total land area it is a big country by any stretch of imagination. Therefore, it is called a sub-continent.

In the matter of population, India is second only to China, India is a densely populated country. This mammoth population is a great problem for India. Although she has rich resources and was once known as "the Golden Sparrow," yet now she is a poor developing country even more than seventy years after attaining Independence, mainly because of this rapid increase in population.

India has made tremendous progress in various fields like agriculture and irrigation, industry, engineering and pharmaceutical goods, in particular, in Information Technology, in Space Research and nuclear science. At the time of Independence, India was a country which depended for most of its necessities on foreign countries. Now, India is making and manufacturing almost everything for its needs— from the smallest pin or needle to the biggest ship, aircraft, atom bomb and even spacecraft.

India has the lofty Himalayas to the north, a large part of which lies within India. In the south, she has the Indian Ocean and the countries like Sri Lanka, Malaysia and Indonesia. India's boundaries touch Bangladesh and Nepal in the north-east, Myanmar and China in the east, Pakistan and Afghanistan in the west-north. She has the Arabian Sea in the west and far at some distance lies the large continent of Africa. The imaginary Equator is situated not very far off from the southernmost tip of India, while the Tropic of Cancer passes through the middle of India in the dry tracts of Rajasthan.

India has a unity in diversity in all respects. She has cold lofty hills of Siachen and Kargil and hot dry regions of Rajasthan. The south, being near the Equator is a hot region almost the whole year.

There is extreme of climate in Punjab, Haryana and most of north India. The Himalayan peaks and some peaks in Himachal Pradesh and Jammu and Kashmir remain covered with snow almost the whole year.

If most of Rajasthan remains a dry desert almost the whole year because of the Tropic of Cancer and the structure of the Aravali hills which are shaped parallel to the direction of the monsoon winds from the Arabian Sea, Asom is wet almost the whole year. Mausinram near Cherapunji which is situated in this state is the wettest place on the earth, recording about 467 inches of rain per year. The Indian people belong to different religions, castes and races. They speak different languages. They wear different dresses. They have different food habits. Yet, they are Indians, first and last.

India is a federation of 29 states and 7 union territories. It has a democratic set-up based on the Parliamentary system of government. It is a republic with the President as the head of the state. The real power lies in the union cabinet headed by the Prime Minister. There are two houses of Parliament—the Lok Sabha, the lower house and the Rajya Sabha, the upper house. The main legislative power lies with the lower house which is elected by the people for a term of five years. There is a similar system in the states. The President is the head of the government, while the Prime Minister and his council of ministers are the elected representatives of the people.

India has a Panchayati system at the grass roots level. There is an independent judiciary to interpret the Constitution which is the longest in the world. There are High Courts at the state level and district and other lower courts at the lower level. There are also municipal corporations in big cities and municipal committees in small towns.

Unfortunately, India has a hostile neighbour who like India is a nuclear power but is always at loggerheads with India. India is the land of great peace-lovers like the Buddha, Guru Nanak and Gandhi. She has friendship with all countries. Only one particular neighbouring state has spurned all her peace offers and the Kashmir problem has become a great headache for India.

About 21.9 per cent of population of India still lives below the poverty line. There are also other problems like unemployment, wide-spread corruption, etc. Indian government is trying to overcome and solve all the problems with the cooperation of the people. Let us hope for the best.

STUDENTS' ROLE IN NATIONAL RECONSTRUCTION

The primary duty of students is to pursue knowledge. As such a student is expected to pursue his aim of gaining knowledge with a single-minded devotion and a spirit of dedication.

However, even studies can be pursued if proper atmosphere for this exists. As such, all sections of society have a duty to maintain calm and congeniality in their homes and elsewhere to let these future leaders of the country do their job diligently.

The Indian students, by and large, did a yeoman's job during the freedom struggle. On the call given by our political leaders, they came out of their institutions and took a major part in the freedom struggle.

After Independence, now the students' role in India is limited to the pursuit of knowledge and taking active part in such national policies as census, pulse polio, T.B., malaria, AIDS, Hepatitis-B and C eradication programmes, as also such programmes and campaigns as Adult Education, literacy, etc.

It is heartening to note that the Indian students have often shown great alertness and enthusiasm in promoting national programmes and policies. They have risen to occasion on such crucial times as the Gujarat earthquake, Orissa supercyclone, floods in different parts of the country, famines in certain areas, controlling of communal riots and other problems.

It is also important that while at school and colleges, the students should also be given some training in certain arts, crafts and simple technologies, such that they develop a scientific bent of mind and shun superstitions and faith in fate. They should be taught the dignity of labour such that they do not go after white collar jobs and have confidence in self-help and self-dependence.

There is no doubt that in the modern world of rising prices yawning unemployment and yawning disparities in incomes and all-pervading atmosphere of tension, stress and strain, angst, multiple dangers even to the existence of mankind on this planet and uncertainty, it is, indeed, very difficult, if not impossible, even for a sincere person, may be a student or anybody else, to deliver the goods in right earnest.

The Gita teaches us that we should do our duty in all circumstances, irrespective of the visible consequences, as the fruit or result is in the hands of God.

It is the duty of a student to pursue his studies and do other national jobs with heart and soul and he should not desist from doing so in any kind of situation.

At any institution, a student must try to develop all round personality by taking part in extramural and cocurricular activities such as speech-making, painting competition, debates, declamation content histrionics, musical concerts, fancy dress show, dance or acting competition, poetical recitation, paper reading, quiz competition, seminars, workshops lectures, social and national campaigns etc. He should not fight shy of doing his duty when he is asked to shoulder some responsibility such as organising a camp, a seminar, a match, a function, etc. Such experiences can prove very useful to him later in life and as such, he can also prove an asset' to the nation.

A student must also take care of his health and character. If the student is healthy, he can study better and come off with flying colours at all examinations. As such, he must take part in sports.

They should work for the nation and try to grow into physically, mentally and emotionally healthy adults such that they can take the reins of the country in the most suitable way as the time comes. They should even be ready to sacrifice for the country, if need be.

THE VALUE OF SPORTS

It is rightly said that all work and no play makes Jack a dull boy.

A student who goes on studying day and night, gets himself reduced to a skeleton. He may shine in studies and win many prizes and scholarships, but without good health, he cannot get real success and happiness in life. A healthy pauper is happier than an unhealthy billionaire or than one as learned as Socrates.

Therefore, even if studies are important, sports have their own value.

Sports provide us the exercise which is necessary and important for health and life. They also make us mentally alert and thus we can concentrate more on any subject.

When we are in the field, we have to play keeping in mind all the rules of the play. Thus, we learn the importance of discipline.

In the field, we have to be alert and practical. In this way, we learn how to act in a practical way in life.

In the playground, we also imbibe certain positive virtues such as team-spirit, sportsmanship, qualities of leadership, taking success and failure with equal equanimity, etc.

Sports and games must be played for the sake of game and not just for success. Of course, we must aspire and make strenuous efforts to get success, but we must not try to defeat our rivals by underhand methods.

In the modern times, the value of sports has been greatly recognized. We have so many sports clubs and organisations at local, state, national and international level. We have sports ministry at the centre.

So far, India has not been a great sports nation in the world. Our performance at the Olympics has often been dismal. In recent times, our teams in several spheres have shown some improvement. Let us hope India will become a great country even in the field of sports in the near future.

GOOD MANNERS

Sometimes, parents advise their children not to play with bad boys.

Who are those bad boys whose company is desired to be shunned? They are, actually just children as all other children. Only they have bad manners. In other words, they don't observe good manners or they don't know what good manners are. May be, they haven't been guided properly by their parents or guardians or they are so headstrong that they haven't learnt to do any good in life nor perhaps they have any inclination to do so.

If good manners are so important, then, of course, they must be learnt and followed.

Good manners sometimes overlap with good habits. Such are rising early in the morning, brushing one's teeth, having a regular bath, putting one neat and clean clothes, polishing one's shoes daily, going to school regularly and punctually, having meals at regular times, not talking while eating, obeying and respecting teachers, parents and elders, reading good books, doing homework regularly, etc.

There is a sort of courtesy which the society expects from us. For instance, if we make frequent but proper use of such words and expressions as 'Please', 'Excuse me', 'Thank you', etc. we lose nothing. These words and expressions cost nothing. We gain a lot in the esteem of others. Others also feel happier.

We should always talk in a polite language. We should never be angry nor ever call anybody names, whatever the provocation. We should be truthful and candid but not blunt. We should not hurt anybody's sentiments. We should never be dishonest or deceitful. We should never say anything irreligious, immoral, unpatriotic, unsocial, irritating or the like.

DISCIPLINE

Discipline is the law of nature. Man is an inseparable part of nature. Hence, he has of necessity, to follow and observe discipline in all walks of life.

Nature follows all its laws very scrupulously. The sun rises in the morning and sets in the evening regularly. The seasons come and go in proper order annually. Day and night alternate each other. The heavenly bodies all observe discipline. Then why should not man?

A man who does not observe discipline has to suffer in life. He has to lead a miserable life. He becomes lethargic and may grow errant or intemperate which are but the impending signs of disaster and misery.

A student who does not go to school or college regularly and punctually, nor does he do his homework with full sincerity, cannot be expected to be a brilliant student. Sometimes, such a student may not even get through his examinations. Thus, ultimately, he has to meet with failure in life when even his nearest friends and relatives foresake him. Then he repents, but that is of no use. It is rightly said, "It is no use crying over spilt milk."

An employee who does not work properly in his office may be sacked any time. In such a case, not only he but also his entire family has to suffer for his indisciplined life.

Sportsmen have to be very particular about discipline. A team, the members of which are not well disciplined, cannot hope to get success in any match. A team has to observe team spirit without ignoring the mandates of the captain.

In the army, discipline is of utmost importance. Discipline is the essence of any good army. An army cannot be just called an army if its soldiers are not well-disciplined. No army can win a battle unless it is highly disciplined.

A farmer who does not sow seeds in the field at the right time and then does not water the plants regularly, cannot hope to get a bumper crop.

Discipline is of utmost importance on the road. One must run one's vehicle in the proper lanes and always keep to the left normally. A careless pedestrian can get crushed under the wheels of a vehicle.

Many people confuse liberty with complete freedom to do anything they like. They think that discipline and liberty are antagonistic to each other. As a matter of fact, liberty and discipline are complementary to each other. One helps the other. No man can hope for any concession regarding liberty from others if he is not ready to give any such concession to others.

Accordingly every right has a corresponding duty. Thus, if we think, we have the right to do something, we are then also under obligation to let others also do the same thing. In this way, though seemingly, discipline and liberty seem to cut each other, in reality they only ensure and guarantee the possibility of the other.

Discipline is said to be broadly of two types :

(i)   Physical discipline

(ii)   Moral (or higher) discipline

Physical discipline may be observed by anybody by just being bold in the face of danger. But moral discipline demands the controlling of emotion and giving up many things like greed, attachment, ego, desire, anger, etc. That is a more difficult task particularly for a worldly man. Only a stoic or a recluse can observe it in letter and spirit.

Certain virtues like truthfulness, honesty, sincerity, unflinching faith in God, patriotism, etc. must also be considered examples of moral discipline. Those who do not get corrupted even in the face of all temptation and allurement must be deemed great and brave souls.

Let us try to develop in us both kinds of discipline. That is easy in childhood and impressionable years of adolescence and youth. A disciplined person is an asset to himself, to his family, to the society, to the nation and to the whole of mankind.

NEW 7 WONDERS OF THE WORLD

On 7/7/7 (a string of sevens) the new seven wonders of the world were announced by the New 7 Wonders Foundation (N7W), a privately funded organization from Zurich in Switzerland. The announcement was made in Lisbon since it was a neutral country because no historical places was a contender for the new seven wonders from the country.

The seven wonders were selected by millions of voters from across the globe by online or via telephone for their countries historical monuments to win and find a place in the new seven wonders of the world. The Seven New Wonders of the World are :

1. Taj Mahal (India) : This sublime mausoleum was built in 17th century by Shah Jahan in memory of his beloved wife Mumtaz Mahal. It is built out of white marble and is the greatest symbol of love and passion. It is regarded as the most excellent piece of Indo-Islamic art.

2. Great Wall of China (China): It was built (220 BC and 1368-1644 AD) to keep invading Mongol tribes out of China. It is the longest man made monument to be visible from space!

3. Ruins of Petra (Jordan): It was the glittering capital of the Nabataean empire of King Arctas IV (9 BC to 40 AD). It had great tunnel construction, theatre and its 42-metre high Hellenistic temple facade on the El-Deir Monastery are impressive examples of Middle Eastern Culture.

4. Roman Colosseum (Rome): An amphitheatre in the centre of Rome was built in (70-82 AD) to celebrate the glory of the Roman Empire. Cruel fights and games used to take place in the area for the joy of the spectators!

5. The Statue of Christ Redeemer (Brazil): A 38 metre tall statue of Jesus built is 1931 stands atop the Carcovado mountain overlooking Rio de Janeiro. It welcomes visitors to Brazil.

6. Incan Emperor Pachacutec (Peru): The 15th century extraordinary settlement was built on the mountain known as Machu Picchu. It is a symbol of dedication and community.

7. Chichen Itza (Mexico): It was built around 500 AD by Mayan rulers in the Yucatan Peninsula of Mexico. Chichen Itza was primarily designed to be a temple city. The Pyramid was the best and stronger of all the structures which still exist there.

❏ ❏ ❏

SECTION B : LETTERS

An Application to the Principal for Leave

To

The Principal,

D.A.V. Higher Secondary School,

Pusa Road, New Delhi

Sir,

I beg to state that I have been suffering from fever for the last two days. My doctor has advised me complete bed rest for a week.

Therefore, I request you to kindly grant me leave for ten days with effect from 9th to the 17th January, (year) __, both days inclusive. A medical certificate is enclosed along with this application.

I shall be grateful to you for your act of kindness in this regard.

Yours obediently,

(Full date)   Vishakha Raj

Encl: One Medical Certificate   Class IX, Section C

Letter to the Principal Requesting for Fee-Concession

To

The Principal,

Govt. Boys Senior Secondary School,

Gole Market, New Delhi.

Sir,

I beg to state that I am a student of class X in your school. I have been studying in your school for five years. I am hardworking and a brilliant student so much so that my teachers can vouch for. I also fair well in extra-curricular activities.

My father was employed in a private company. Recently he met with a serious accident and subsequently lost his job. Now my brother is the only earning member. He is a clerk and earns a low salary just enough to meet our essential expenses. There is no one else to support us.

I, therefore, request you to kindly grant me fee-concession in order to enable me to continue with my studies.

I shall be grateful if you do the needful.

Thanking you,

Yours faithfully,
Supreet Behl
Class X, Section B

(Full date)

An Application to the Principal for the Certificates

To

The Principal,

Ramjas Girls Senior Secondary School,

Pusa Road, New Delhi.

Madam,

I beg to state that I am a student of class IX in your school. I am a regular student and obtained II position in class VIII. I have also won many prizes in extra-curricular activities of the school.

My father who is working with the Central Government has been transferred to another city. We shall leave this city by the end of this month. It is not possible for me to stay here alone.

Therefore, I request you to kindly issue me the necessary Transfer Certificate and Character Certificate which will enable me to seek admission in the other school.

I have paid all my school dues and returned all the books I had, to the library.

I shall be grateful if you kindly issue the certificates by the end of next week.

Thanking you,

Yours obediently,
Pratiksha Roy
Class IX, Section A

(Full date)

Letter to the Principal for Seeking Admission to School Hostel

To

The Principal,

Delhi Public School,

Mathura Road, New Delhi.

Sir,

I beg to state that I am a XII standard student of your school.

My father, who is an employee of the Government of India, has been transferred to another State. He will leave Delhi on the 26th of this month to take up his new assignment in time. All the members of the family will accompany him but I have to remain here in order to complete my final year in school and sit for the Board Examination to be held in the month of March.

There is no one with whom I can stay after they leave and I shall have to discontinue my studies unless I am admitted to the hostel.

I request you to kindly admit me as a boarder in the school hostel to enable me to continue my studies undisturbed.

I shall be grateful to you for your act of kindness in this regard.

Yours obediently,

Neeru Sood

(Full date)   Class XII, Section D

Letter to Your Father Requesting an Increase in Monthly Allowance

(Full address of the writer, and date)

My dear Father,

I have not heard from you or mother since I returned to my hostel after winter vacations. I hope everybody at home is doing well.

I am fine and busy with my studies as examinations are drawing near. I am getting along well except that our hostel charges have been raised with effect from this month and I am in want of money. Moreover, the prices of commodities have gone up and I am not able to make my own purchase of books and eatables.

Father, you know I am not a spendthrift. I really need more money now. I request you to increase my monthly allowance reasonably. I eagerly await your reply.

My deepest regards to you and mother and love to Ruchi.

Your affectionate son,
Sushant

(Full name and address of the recipient)

Letter to a Cousin Congratulating Him on His Engagement

(Full address of the writer, and date)

Dear Vaibhav,

It has really been long that I heard from you and when I did it was a pleasant surprise. The news of your engagement to Ruchi Kalra has made me really happy. Accept my heartily congratulations.

You always wanted to marry a person who is well educated and takes keen interest in the affairs even outside home. As far as I know Miss Ruchi is a famous columnist, so this engagement should be the fulfilment of your desire. I hope that she also wished to marry an officer with a pleasing personality like your's. She is lucky to have such a polished person like you as her life partner.

Let me know when will be the grand day that you two shall become man and wife. I look forward to the day. May be, I get a chance to visit you next month.

Congratulating you once again,

Yours lovingly,
Tripti

(Full name and address of the recipient)

Letter to the Executive Councillor Requesting Him to be the Chief Guest at the Annual Day Function of Your School

(Full address of the writer, and date)

To

Hon'ble Executive Councillor,

Delhi.

Respected Sir,

As the School Prefect I, the undersigned, beg to request you on behalf of the students and the staff of the school to preside over our

Annual Day Function to be held on 17th September (year) at 6:30 pm in our School auditorium.

Our country is passing through a trying phase. We wish to inform you that we have collected ₹ 24,000/- (Twenty four thousand only) from students, parents, friends and staff members for the Prime Minister's Relief Fund.

The Annual Day Function shall begin with an Introductory Welcome Speech followed by a variety of cultural programme including fancy dress competition and a fashion show of traditional Indian dresses especially presented by our primary school section. Then the prizes will be distributed. The function will end with the Principal's speech and a vote of thanks to the Chief Guest. The whole programme shall be for three hours duration.

All the students of the school are eager to meet you. We hope you will kindly find time to grace the occasion with your presence. Hoping to receive your confirmation at an early date.

Yours faithfully,
Shikha Sharma

Letter to Your Father Telling Him What You Wish to do After Completing School

(Full address of the writer, and date)

My Dear Father,

Received your affectionate letter stating your concern for my future. My Annual Examinations are drawing near and I am studying hard so that I can secure a good percentage of marks.

Father, you have wished me to join your business like my elder brother. But I am not interested in the sale and purchase of garments. I find it dull and boring with hardly anything concrete to be achieved except rich profits. I desire to earn fame in the noble profession of love. I wish to become a doctor and serve the poor section of our society. Our country needs good and able doctors and I want to be one of them. Ever since the death of my best friend due to the rude behaviour of the doctor and inefficient work of the nurses after he had met with an accident, I had decided to become a doctor who is patient-caring and quick in saving lives. I want to become a doctor who is sought, admired and trusted.

I hope you will approve of my wish and help me to realise my aim of life. I shall await your reply which I expect shall liven my spirits further to attain success in my chosen career.

My deepest regards to you, mother and brother.

Your affectionate son,

Gaurav

(Full name and address of the recipient)

Letter to a Friend Congratulating Him on His Selection in NDA Examination

(Full address of the writer, and date)

My dear Anubhav,

I am very much delighted to learn about your selection in the National Defence Academy, Khadakvasla. You shall soon begin a new life and your career shall shine brightly if you put your heart and soul into it.

I heartily congratulate you on your brilliant success. Your hard and sincere efforts have crowned you with glory. I can imagine your excitement at ranking 5th in merit when I myself was thrilled to learn about your result. I am really proud of you. At last you have fulfilled the dream of your parents.

I shall visit you shortly. We shall spend some time together to celebrate your achievement.

I congratulate you once again and wish you all the best for the future.

Yours sincerely,

William

(Full name and address of the recipient)

Letter to a Cousin Inviting Her to Spend Vacation

(Full address of the writer, and date)

My dear Srishti

It is almost a year now that we have not met each other. The Summer Vacation begins next month. My neighbourhood friend Mitu will also be here for two months. She will not be visiting her uncle this year. I sincerely wish for your presence here. We three will have a pleasant time together. My parents shall also be glad with your visit.

Let me know your vacation plans. I look forward to an affirmative reply.

Convey my best regards to Uncle and Aunty and love to little Rishi.

Yours sincerely,

Pooja

(Full name and address of the recipient)

Letter to Your Grandfather Requesting Him to Send You Birthday Present of Your Choice

(Full address of the writer, and date)

My dear Grandpa,

I received your affectionate letter in which you have mentioned that you are planning to send me a new bicycle as my birthday present. You never forget my birthday and I am proud of all your lovely gifts.

I thank you for your gift but, dear grandpa, I wish to tell you that what I really need is a good wrist-watch. My present bicycle is in a fit condition and I do not need a new one right now. I have lost my wrist-watch by accident. I tried to search it everywhere possible but in vain. So I thought it better to inform you about my requirement. I hope you do not mind my being so outspoken regarding my choice.

I want you to attend my birthday party. Moreover, eight months have passed since you visited us last. Please do not disappoint me. I shall wait for you.

With regards,

Your affectionate granddaughter,

Chanchal

(Full name and address of the recipient)

Letter to a Sports Dealer for Supply of Sports Goods

To
M/s Rathi Sports,
Jhandewalan Extension,
New Delhi.

Sir,

I am pleased to inform you that the residents of my colony have recently formed a Sports Club. The Club's Committee has approved of the sports goods as mentioned below. As a Secretary of the Sports Club I request you to supply us the mentioned articles as early as possible:

Articles	Quantity	Brand
Cricket bat	4	SSS
Cricket leather ball	6	Superior
Carrom board (with coins)	1	Mayur
Volleyball	1	Rajah

Kindly send the bills along with the articles through your representative so that we can make the payment.

Thanking you,

Yours faithfully,
Sunil Wadhavan

Letter to the Municipal Authorities Complaining About Bad Roads and Lights in Your Locality

To
The Municipal Commissioner,
New Delhi.

Sir,

I wish to bring to your knowledge that the residents of my locality are suffering due to bad roads. The rainy season has led to many pot-holes on the road. They are becoming a good breeding ground for mosquitoes. Water collects therein and the depth of the holes cannot be known. As such almost all vehicles go through a bumpy uncomfortable journey. Moreover, at night lack of proper streetlight makes driving home difficult.

I, therefore, request you to kindly attend to the problems as soon as possible. Your early action in this regard shall be highly appreciated.

Thanking you,

Yours sincerely,
Hitesh Malik

Letter to the Editor About Frequent Breakdowns of Electricity in Your Locality

To

The Editor,

The Times of India,

New Delhi.

Sir,

Kindly permit me to draw the attention of the concerned authorities towards the frequent breakdowns of electricity in my locality through the columns of your esteemed daily.

The electricity goes off and on for hours. On an average we have the benefit of electricity for just two or three hours a day. This is causing great inconvenience to the residents. Moreover, it is the time for examinations and the children are affected the most. The various complaints by the members of the Colony Association have fallen on deaf ears.

The electricity authorities are requested to take immediate measures to repair the wiring defects which cause these breakdowns.

Thanking you,

Yours faithfully,
Vijaya Bharadwaj

Letter to the Editor About Irregular Water Supply in Your Locality

To

The Editor,

The Hindustan Times,

New Delhi.

Sir,

I request you to permit me to draw the attention of the Municipal Corporation of Delhi towards the irregular and inadequate water supply in our locality through the columns of Action Line in your esteemed daily.

As President of the Locality Association I have complained to the Corporation many time but in vain. Water is one of the basic necessities. We pay a good amount of taxes and in return expect efficient services by the Corporation.

There is frequent breakdown of water supply that causes a lot of inconvenience. The working section of our residents are very often delayed for work as they have to stand in the long queue at the main water tap. Unfortunately, the pressure of water at the main water tap is also very low.

Many a time the water we get is dirty and muddy which is not fit for drinking. Our children fall an easy prey to illness. The summer season has become a curse to the residents of this locality.

The Corporation Authorities are requested to take immediate measures to ensure regular water supply. Their early action will be appreciated.

Thanking you,

Yours Faithfully,
Naresh Nagmani

Letter to the Post Master Complaining About Irregular Delivery of the Post

To
The Post Master,
GPO Karol Bagh,
New Delhi.

Sir,

I wish to bring to your kind notice the problems I am facing due to irregular delivery of the post.

Today I received my Application Form for admission to Medical College. The last date of submission of the form is 18th Feb (year) i.e., tomorrow. I have no time to enrol myself for the Entrance Examination. Only if the postal service had been regular I would have received the form a week back. The stamp on the envelope clearly shows the date of receival as 10th Feb (year). This is due to the negligence of the

Postman in our area who is not regular. He comes only for two days in a week. At times he is missing for days. When asked about the irregularity he was rude in reply.

The Postman is careless and many a time I have received letters in my house belonging to some other person. He throws the mail in front of the door instead of putting it in the mail box meant for the purpose. As such, many of our letters have been misplaced.

You are requested to kindly change the Postman or to instruct the present one to perform his duty properly. I hope you will take an early action.

Yours sincerely,

Manu Gupta

Letter to the Chairman of Delhi Transport Undertaking Requesting Him to Provide a Permanent Bus Stop Near Your Colony

(Full address of the writer, and date)

To

The Chairman,

Delhi Transport Undertaking,

Sir,

As a Secretary of the AGCR Colony's Welfare Association I request you, on behalf of all the residents, to provide a permanent bus stop near our colony.

Our locality consists of numerous office-goers who have to walk the distance of almost a kilometre to the nearest bus stop. People have to face a lot of inconvenience, specially during the night. Walking with ladies and children is all the more risky. All the residents shall be really grateful if immediate arrangements are made to provide this essential facility.

An early action will be highly appreciated.

Thanking you,

Yours faithfully,

Nahar Singh

Letter to the SHO of your town complaining him about the theft of your motorbike.

Examination Hall
XYZ City
Date ....

To
The SHO,
Sadar Police Station
ABC
Sir,

I wish to draw your attention towards the theft of my black motorbike bearing number plate 48E 4949. Yesterday I parked it outside the Plaza Shopping Complex. I locked it properly and went inside the Plaza to make some purchases. I spent not more than fifteen minutes there and as I went outside the Plaza I found my motorbike missing. I asked many persons around if they could tell me anything about its whereabouts. But none of them seemed to have any useful information about it.

I request you to look into the matter and solve my problem at your earliest.

Yours faithfully,

(PK KAPOOR)

Letter to the President of the Municipal Committee of your town requesting him to provide a park for children in your locality.

72, Lovely Dham,
Dev Nagar, Near Gol Bagh (City)
Date ....

To
The President,
Municipal Committee,
.... City.

Dear Sir,

Reg: Providing a park for children.

The Dev Nagar colony in which I am living has a population of no less than five thousand people. A large majority of the populace comprises children.

All of us know that the major interest of children is in playing. But, unfortunately, there is not a single park for children in this area. The poor children have to play on the roads and in busy streets which is so dangerous.

It is, therefore, requested that a lovely park for children should be provided in this locality. There are a number of plots of land lying vacant. One or more of these may be acquired for the purpose.

Thank you.

Yours faithfully,
(Ram Kapoor)

Letter to the Chief Medical Officer of your district suggesting that it is the right time to launch a drive against Dengue.

89, Gobind Street,
Karnal.
Date ....

To
The Chief Medical Officer,
Karnal.
Dear Sir,

Reg: Drive against Dengue.

I have noted with great disgust that for the last many years the deadly disease of dengue has been taking a heavy toll of human life in our district. No doubt, a drive against this disease is started vigorously every year, but it is always done when the disease is already in full bloom.

I, therefore, suggest that a drive against dengue should be started right from now. It is because rains start in early July and they bring in their train mosquitoes which spread the deadly disease. Morever, these days when summer is at its peak, people make the maximum use of desert coolers and we know that mosquitoes flourish in the stagnant containers of these coolers.

So, I hope, keeping in view my request, advice or suggestion, whatever you might like to take it, steps will be taken immediately to prevent the occurrence of this disease this year and ever afterwards.

Thank you.

Yours faithfully,
(Gulshan Kumar)

❑ ❑ ❑

www.ingramcontent.com/pod-product-compliance
Lightning Source LLC
Chambersburg PA
CBHW050500080326
40788CB00001B/3923